School to Work:
Research on Programs in the United States

The Stanford Series on Education and Public Policy

General Editor: Professor Henry M. Levin, School of Education, Stanford University

The purpose of this series is to address major issues of educational policy as they affect and are affected by political, social and economic issues. It focuses on both the consequences of education for economic, political and social outcomes as well as the influences of the economics, political and social climate on education. It is particularly concerned with addressing major educational issues and challenges within this framework, and a special effort is made to evaluate the various educational alternatives on the policy agenda or to develop new ones that might address the educational challenges before us. All of the volumes are to be based upon original research and/or competent syntheses of the available research on a topic.

The Stanford Series on Education & Public Policy: 17

School to Work:
Research on Programs in the United States

David Stern, Neal Finkelstein, James R. Stone III,
John Latting and Carolyn Dornsife

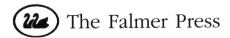 The Falmer Press

(A member of the Taylor & Francis Group)
London • Washington, D.C.
for the National Center for Research in Vocational Education

UK The Falmer Press, 4 John Street, London WC1N 2ET
USA The Falmer Press, Taylor & Francis Inc., 1900 Frost Road, Suite 101, Bristol, PA 19007

First published in 1995

A catalogue record for this book is available from the British Library

Library of Congress Cataloging-in-Publication Data are available on request

ISBN 0 7507 0428 4 cased
ISBN 0 7507 0429 2 paper

Jacket design by Caroline Archer

Typeset in 11/13pt Garamond by
Graphicraft Typesetters Ltd., Hong Kong.

Printed in Great Britain by Burgess Science Press, Basingstoke on paper which has a specified pH value on final paper manufacture of not less than 7.5 and is therefore 'acid free'.

Contents

Contents

In memory of Charles S. Benson

Scholar and Mentor

Acknowledgments

This report was prepared for submission by the National Center for Research in Vocational Education, of the University of California at Berkeley, under section 404 (b)(2) of the 1990 Amendments to the Carl D. Perkins Vocational and Applied Technology Education Act. We are grateful to Paul Barton, Stephen Hamilton, Jerry Hayward, James Rosenbaum, Laurence Steinberg, two anonymous reviewers, and especially David Boesel for helpful comments on earlier drafts. Work on this report was supported by the US Department of Education through the Office of Vocational and Adult Education, the National Center on the Educational Quality of the Workforce, and the National Assessment of Vocational Education, and by the National Research Council of the National Academy of Science. However, the conclusions and opinions stated here are the authors' alone, and do not necessarily reflect the views or positions of the US Department of Education or the National Academy of Science.

List of Figures and Tables

Figures

Tables

Executive Summary

Encouraged by federal legislation, states and localities in the US are designing new school-to-work systems. This report is intended to assist these design efforts by presenting the results of research on existing school-to-work programs.

The discussion begins with a brief overview of the difficulties encountered by many young people in making the transition from school to work. A chronic scarcity of career jobs is part of the problem. Reduced employment in manufacturing during the 1980s further diminished the prospects of men without any post-secondary education. The increase in relative earnings of four-year college graduates in the 1980s, along with evidence of a growing difference in earnings for high school graduates who are more competent in mathematics, point to an increased demand for mental ability in the workplace. One implication is that school-to-work systems should prepare students not only for their first full-time jobs, but also for continued learning and career transitions throughout their working lives.

Prominent among ideas for improving the school-to-work system are the integration of the academic and occupational curriculum, the linking of school with a structured work experience, and the creation of formal connections between secondary and post-secondary education. Each of these represents a formidable challenge. There is some disagreement about whether school-to-work programs should link high school to four-year colleges, or only to two-year post-secondary institutions. Given the greater earnings of four-year college graduates, school-to-work programs risk being regarded as second-best unless they clearly keep the four-year college option open.

School-to-work programs are classified here in two main categories. School-*and*-work arrangements allow students to work and attend school during the same time period. Apprenticeship and cooperative education are examples. School-*for*-work programs provide instruction with the express purpose of preparing students for work. Traditional and newer forms of vocational education are the main examples in this second category.

School-and-work programs that exist in many high schools and secondary vocational centers include cooperative education, new youth apprenticeships, and school-based enterprises. Cooperative education (co-op) has been practiced in the US for more than eighty years. It involves students in paid work that is related to their field of study. Evaluations have indicated that co-op is successful in creating a stronger connection between school and work in students' minds, and in improving attitudes toward both school and work. However, co-op students have not generally been found to obtain higher earnings after leaving high school, unless they continue working for their co-op employer. One possible reason for this may be that co-op does not provide any certification that is widely recognized by employers. Therefore, co-op graduates who are not offered permanent jobs by their co-op employers may not obtain much advantage in the labor market from their co-op experience. If this explanation is correct, creation of skill standards for specific occupations and industries would help co-op graduates (in addition to graduates of other work-related programs) to convert their experience into higher earnings.

Co-op in high school has mainly been used as part of vocational education. Although some participants have gone to college, the proportion has been smaller than among other high school graduates.

High schools are now becoming involved in new youth apprenticeship initiatives. Like co-op, these link high school with a structured work experience, but they are also trying to create a clearer path to post-secondary education, in addition to providing occupational certification. No evidence is yet available on the effects of these initiatives, though the first evaluations will soon be forthcoming.

More widespread than youth apprenticeship is school-based enterprise, which involves students in producing goods or services for sale or use to people other than the participating students themselves. Frequently observed activities of high school enterprise are house building, school stores, restaurants, child care, and car repair. Working in a school-based enterprise may provide some of the same benefits for students as working in a non-school enterprise, and may be more conducive to learning, since school-based enterprises exist for educational purposes. However, there has been virtually no systematic evaluation of these programs.

Many high school students are also employed in jobs that are not supervised by the school in any way. In fact, students participating in these do-it-yourself school-and-work arrangements vastly outnumber those involved in school-supervised or school-based work experience. Students who work during high school obtain higher earnings in the first few years after leaving high school. In addition, students who work only a moderate number of hours per week have been found to perform better in school than those who do not work at all. However, students who work more hours per week perform less well in high school and obtain less post-secondary education. It is difficult to say how much these correlations represent the effect of working, or how much they reflect pre-existing differences among students. An important question, as yet unanswered, is whether providing some school supervision for jobs that are not now supervised by the school would mitigate some of the negative relationship between working and school performance.

School-and-work programs that are common in two-year colleges include cooperative education and apprenticeship. There has not been much evaluation of co-op in two-year colleges, as opposed to four-year colleges, where co-op has a different format and often a different purpose. The few evaluations in two-year colleges suggest results similar to co-op in high schools. Two-year colleges have also played a substantial role in providing the classroom component of traditional apprenticeship programs, and they are beginning to become involved in new youth apprenticeship initiatives.

In addition to these school-and-work programs, which involve students in school and work concurrently, vocational education at the secondary and post-secondary level also tries to create a strong sequential connection between school and work. Evidence on high school programs is mixed, but one clear finding is that the payoff is greater when vocational graduates find work related to their field of training. Students who complete two-year college degrees on average receive significantly greater earnings than students with high school diplomas only, but statistical studies that control for student background have found this effect only for associate degrees in math and science, or for women in vocational fields. Estimates of the effects of taking courses but not completing a degree in a two-year college are highly variable. Effects of proprietary schools appear to be positive but smaller than two-year college degrees after age 30.

Prompted in part by the 1990 Amendments to the Carl Perkins Act, vocational education is changing. One major new initiative is the integration of academic and vocational curriculum. Evaluations of five programs summarized here have found some positive effects on students' school performance and retention, but there has not yet been much evaluation of effects on students' subsequent employment.

The 1990 Amendments to the Perkins Act also provided new federal support for tech-prep programs, which create a coherent sequence of courses linking high schools and (usually two-year) colleges. Some new youth apprenticeship programs can be described as tech-prep with a work-based learning component. There has been some research on implementation of tech-prep, but evaluations of its effects on students are still in progress.

Although this is a review of research on transition to work from school, we include a summary of selected studies of programs for young people who are not attending school. The Job Corps stands out as having the most positive evaluation results, but this was a quasi-experimental evaluation. No random-assignment evaluations have found any program to be effective in increasing the earnings of out-of-school youth.

There have been numerous studies of school-to-work programs, but the research is still limited in several respects. Very few evaluations have used random-assignment methods, so the possibility of selection bias is ever-present. Also, most programs are complex, and when a program is found to have positive effects it is usually impossible to know exactly which element or elements are responsible. Finally, there is also a lack of evidence about the effect of a comprehensive school-to-work system; testing alternative systems in different localities would be a useful undertaking.

A concluding section considers implications for states and localities designing new school-to-work systems. A strategic question is whether to design these systems only for students who are not expected to attend college, or to include also students who may go on to a four-year college or university. Keeping the four-year college option open avoids the risk of stigma, and avoids limiting students' future career prospects. On the other hand, keeping this option open adds to the complexity of designing new school-based curriculum and work-based learning arrangements. Though design and implementation are difficult, new school-to-work systems can potentially help young people not only to find their first full-time jobs, but also to acquire a capacity for learning while they work, which will help them throughout their working lives.

1   The Transition Problem, and Proposed Solutions

The transition from school to career in the US is often messy, takes a long time, and for some people never succeeds. Most young Americans now start working at paid jobs while they are in high school, but these jobs are seldom connected to their studies or career aspirations. Most high school graduates go directly to college, where a large majority hold paid jobs, but again most of these jobs do not contribute to their education. After leaving school, with or without a diploma, most young people spend a number of years 'floundering' from one job to another, often with occasional spells of unemployment in between. Even by age 40, many have not found stable employment. New school-to-work initiatives are intended, in part, to prevent this evident waste of human resources.

Floundering Youth in the US Labor Market

Unemployment rates remain high for young people right out of high school. As of mid-1993 the unemployment rate among 18 and 19-year-olds stood at 19 per cent nationally. Among 20 to 24-year-olds it was 11 per cent, compared to 5.7 per cent among job seekers aged 25 to 54 (US Department of Labor, 1993a, table A-8). High unemployment rates for young workers in 1993 were still showing the effects of the 1990/91 recession, but even during the relatively prosperous period from 1985 to 1989 the unemployment rate among teenagers (age 16 to 19) never fell below 15 per cent.

The National Longitudinal Survey of Youth has revealed that, between the ages of 18 and 27, the average high school graduate who did not enroll in post-secondary education held nearly six different jobs and experienced between four and five spells of unemployment. While spending a total of 387 weeks employed during those years, the average graduate also spent almost thirty-five weeks unemployed (Veum and Weiss, 1993).

High unemployment rates for young workers take a toll on career development. There is ample evidence that teenagers who acquire more work experience earn higher wages in subsequent years (Meyer and Wise, 1982; Ellwood, 1982; Lynch, 1989; d'Amico and Maxwell, 1990). D'Amico and Maxwell show that lack of work experience among young black males accounts for about half of the difference between their wages and those of young white males five years after graduating from high school.

During the 1970s the perceived cause of youth unemployment was excess supply, stemming from the large number of baby boomers then entering the labor market. However, in the 1980s the youth labor market was occupied by the baby bust generation born in the 1960s. Concern about a surplus of young workers turned to worry about a shortage of young people qualified to fill jobs in the new service economy (Johnston and Packer, 1987). This anxiety was prompted not only by the smaller size of the youth cohort but also by the perceived inadequacy of their knowledge, skills, and attitudes (for example, Committee for Economic Development, 1985).

According to this latter view, youth unemployment is attributable in large part to lack of qualification for existing jobs. In a 1991 Harris poll, employers reported that they have to turn down five of every six young people who apply for a job.

> The survey of officials of 402 companies found 30 per cent giving a positive rating for recent high school graduates' ability to read well, and 22 per cent crediting students with having learned basic mathematics. But only 13 per cent said recent graduates could write well, and just 10 per cent believed they had 'learned to solve complex problems'. (Weisman, 1991, p. 5)

These explanations for youth unemployment stress the supply side, as opposed to the demand side, of the labor market. An alternative explanation is that employers offer too few steady jobs with career prospects. As a result, many young people have to go through a 'floundering' period (Osterman, 1989; Hamilton, 1990): drifting from one short-term job to another, quitting or being laid off, staying out of the labor market for a while or searching for work in haphazard fashion, and accepting the next job offer that comes by. Although the US does not always exceed other countries in youth unemployment — for example, mid-1993 unemployment rates for 16–24-year-olds were 23 per cent in

Table 1: Percentage of workers with 0–4 years tenure, US and six other countries

Country	Age group	Year	Male	Female
Finland	35–39	1985	33.6	41.0
France	35–39	1986	21.7	27.2
Germany	35–39	1984	27.5	38.4
Japan	35–39	1984	16.5	45.3
Netherlands	35–39	1985	24.2	45.2
Spain	35–39	1987	26.6	36.2
US	37–40	1983	39.5	58.3

France, 17 per cent in Britain, and 20 per cent for the twelve nation European Community as a whole (Riding, 1993) — the degree of job instability among young people is exceptionally high in the US. Among 20–24-year-olds in the mid-1980s who had less than five years of tenure with their current employer, the proportion who were still working for the same employer five years later was smaller in the US than in Finland, France, Germany, Japan, the Netherlands, or Spain (OECD, 1994, Chart 6.4). (These are the only other countries for which comparable data were available.)

The lack of steady, career jobs in the US affects mature workers, too. Americans continue to flounder in the labor market longer than their counterparts in other countries. Table 1 shows the percentage of workers in their late thirties who had been with their current employer less than five years, computed from Current Population Survey data in the US and from comparable data in other countries where available (OECD, 1993, tables 4.3 and 4.4). Among both males and females the percentage with short job tenure was largest in the US, despite the fact that the age group shown for the US was slightly older than for the other countries. It is worth noting that the US cohort shown in table 1 would have finished high school between 1961 and 1964, when average scores on Scholastic Aptitude Tests were at their all-time peak. Yet, in the middle years of their working lives, fewer of these Americans were established in long-term jobs than their agemates elsewhere.

High rates of unemployment among American youth, and large proportions of mid-career workers who have not established a long-lasting relationship with their employers, might conceivably reflect unwillingness of American workers to attach themselves to a job. But if this were true, and if employers preferred to have long-term relationships, then there ought to be a bonus for employees who stay longer. In fact, however, the actual salary increment associated with longer tenure is not especially large in the US, compared with Japan, for instance (Hashimoto and Raisian, 1985; Mincer and Higuchi, 1988).

In addition to chronically high unemployment, young people right out of high school also experienced reduced earnings in the 1980s compared to the 1970s, despite the smaller numbers of youth in the labor market. While real earnings of American workers in all age groups declined during the 1980s (Katz and Murphy, 1992; Levy and Murnane, 1992), the drop was steepest among younger workers (US Department of Labor, 1993b). Data from the National Longitudinal Surveys of young workers in the early 1970s (from the cohorts of young men and young women) and the late 1980s (from the youth cohort) permit a comparison between the earnings of recent high school graduates in these two time periods. In their fifth year out of high school, males who graduated in the 1970s earned on average $12.62 an hour in 1991 dollars, but those who graduated in the 1980s earned $9.17 (about 27 per cent less). Female high school graduates earned $8 an hour in 1991 dollars during their fifth year out of high school in the 1970s, but those who graduated in the 1980s took in about fifty cents less, a reduction of about 6 per cent. Unless the skills of male high school graduates deteriorated more than those of their female classmates, the asymmetry between males and females seems to point to demand, rather than supply, factors. In particular, reduction in traditionally male manufacturing jobs diminished the number of high-wage opportunities for male high school graduates, but growth in secretarial jobs traditionally held by females sustained the earnings of female high school graduates.

The operation of demand factors is also evident in the higher relative earnings of college graduates compared to high school graduates (Katz and Murphy, 1992; Levy and Murnane, 1992). The US Department of Labor (1993b) analysis of longitudinal data found that male graduates of four-year colleges in the 1980s earned 13 per cent less in real hourly wages five years after graduation, compared to male college graduates in the 1970s. In percentage terms, this reduction was less than half the loss in real hourly wages for male high school graduates. Among females, real hourly wages for college graduates five years after graduation were actually higher in the 1980s than in the 1970s. Unemployment rates for college graduates also stayed low during the 1980s, in contrast to rising unemployment among high school graduates and dropouts (Freeman, 1991) — further evidence of shifting demand in favor of college-educated workers.

The gain in relative earnings of college graduates compared to high school graduates is widely interpreted as an indication of greater demand for mental skill in the workplace. Some additional evidence comes from a study by Murnane, Willett and Levy (1992). Using 1970s data from the National Longitudinal Study of the High School Class of

1972, and 1980s data from the National Longitudinal Survey of Youth Labor Market Experience, they compared the correlation between test scores in mathematics and hourly wages five years after leaving high school, for graduates who did not attend college. They found a significantly higher payoff to mathematical proficiency in the 1980s than in the 1970s.

In summary, the scarcity of stable employment in the US has made it difficult for young people to find career jobs right after high school. They have had to spend several years floundering in the labor market, and many do not succeed in finding steady jobs even by age 40. Employment prospects for male high school graduates grew still worse in the 1980s, as the number of manufacturing jobs diminished. An apparent increase in the payoff to mental proficiency during the 1980s indicates that high school must help students learn to think if graduates are to qualify for good jobs.

One immediate implication is that the success of a school-to-work program cannot be judged simply by attainment of a full-time job. Young people usually do not stay in their first full-time job. School-to-work transition must therefore be seen as a process that occurs over a period of years. It usually begins with part-time jobs during high school, often includes work combined with post-secondary education immediately after high school, and may also involve periods of further schooling later on. Successful school-to-work transition does not mean that individuals leave school abruptly, or forever. It means that they are able to find and keep the kind of jobs they want, possibly with the aid of continued or intermittent schooling along the way. School-to-work programs must therefore aim to do more than qualify students for their first full-time job. Programs must also seek to ensure that students acquire the knowledge and skill necessary to change jobs and continue learning throughout their working lives.

Elements of School-to-Work Programs

School-to-work programs could conceivably include any and all efforts that contribute to successful school-to-work transition. This definition would encompass all kinds of schooling and non-school education that help in any way to prepare for working life.

However, the definition adopted here is narrower and more manageable. It equates school-to-work with school *for* work — that is, education and training programs in which preparation for work is explicitly a major purpose. Furthermore, baccalaureate and advanced degree programs are not discussed here. The focus is on work-preparation programs that serve students in high schools or non-baccalaureate post-secondary institutions, or out-of-school youth.

A key element of many, though not all, school-to-work programs is that they combine school *and* work during the same period of time. This may mean some hours of work each day, some days of work during the week, or some weeks working during the year. Combining school and work serves two purposes. First, it may help young people learn skills and knowledge to qualify for a full-time job in the near future. Second, it may give them the experience of using work to foster their own learning, and thus contribute to their capacity for change and continued growth in the longer run.

Specifically, among the main programs discussed here are cooperative education, youth apprenticeship, other work experience, school-based enterprise, tech-prep, career academies, and school-to-apprenticeship. Combining school and work is an important element of all of these except tech-prep. These school-and-work programs are discussed in Chapters 2 and 3. Tech-prep is discussed in Chapter 4, along with other school-for-work programs.

According to a survey of secondary schools and two-year public post-secondary institutions conducted for the National Assessment of Vocational Education (NAVE), the estimated percentage of US secondary schools, including comprehensive high schools and vocational schools, that offered each program in 1990/91 was (Stern, 1992a):

	%
cooperative education	49
other work experience	34
school-based enterprise	19
tech-prep	7
school-to-apprenticeship	6
youth apprenticeship	2

The NAVE survey did not specifically ask whether secondary schools operated career academies, but it is known from other sources (Stern, Raby and Dayton, 1992) that in 1990/91 there were approximately 100 career academies, representing less than 1 per cent of the nation's secondary schools.

Figure 1 lists major features of these programs. Some features are present by definition, and are therefore said to appear 'always'. For example, a program would not (or should not) be called co-op or youth apprenticeship if it did not include structured work-based learning

Figure 1: *Approximate relative frequency of features in school-to-work programs* (A = always, U = usually, S = sometimes, R = rarely)

Program feature	Co-op	School-based enter-prise	Tech-prep	School-to-appren-ticeship	Youth appren-ticeship	Career acade-mies
Structured work-based learning while in school	A	U	R	S	A	R
School curriculum builds on work experience	U	S	R	R	U	S
Work experience is paid	A	R	R	U	A	U
Employers provide financial support	A	R	R	U	A	A
Program arranges student work placement	U	A	R	U	U	U
Employer involvement in curriculum design	S	S	U	R	U	U
Integrated academic and vocational curriculum	R	S	U	S	U	A
Formal link to post-secondary education	R	R	A	S	U	S
Employment/college counseling	S	R	U	S	S	S
Pre-11th grade academic preparation	S	R	S	R	R	U
Pre-11th grade career exploration	U	R	S	R	U	U
Targets at-risk or non-college bound students	U	S	R	S	S	S
Students have mentors from outside school	S	R	R	S	U	U
Occupational certification	R	R	S	A	A	R

while in school. However, the frequency of most other features in practice is not known. Local authorities have wide discretion in designing programs and deciding what to call them. Figure 1 thus offers only a fuzzy profile of each program, based on published accounts, interviews, and the authors' experience of what 'usually', 'sometimes' or 'rarely' exists. Appendix A supplements this general description with a listing of thirty specific school-to-work projects in particular localities, and provides additional detail about programmatic features from published descriptions and telephone interviews. Appendix B gives the full names and geographic locations of these thirty examples. For an informative set of case studies, see Pauly, Kopp and Haimson (1994).

Three of the programmatic features in figure 1 are especially important in determining the nature of the program and the kinds of students who participate. These three are also among the required elements of programs to be supported by the 1994 School-to-Work Opportunities Act. They are:

- integration of school-based and work-based learning;
- combined academic and vocational curriculum; and
- linking of secondary and post-secondary education.

A structured work-based learning experience is seen as grounding students' coursework in the practical reality of production, and preparing them for lifelong learning in the context of work. Integration of classroom-based and work-based learning is the essence of apprenticeship. However, formal apprenticeships in the US generally take people in their late twenties or older, not high school students. The absence of apprenticeship opportunities for high school students is what motivates the current attempts to create new 'youth apprenticeships', 'career pathways' or 'career majors'. Prior to the current youth apprenticeship initiative, the program that most closely integrated work-based and school-based learning in American high schools and two-year colleges was cooperative education ('co-op'). The research on co-op is summarized later in this report.

Both apprenticeship and co-op offer paid employment linked to students' schoolwork, and organize students' learning on the job by means of written training plans and written agreements with employers to provide the necessary supervision and instruction. School-based enterprises also provide a structured learning experience in the workplace, but usually the work takes place on school premises and students are not paid. Career academies ordinarily arrange paid jobs for students related to their field of study, but typically there are no written training agreements or training plans. In a school-to-apprenticeship program the structured work-based learning would usually not begin until after high school graduation. Some individual tech-prep programs may include structured learning in the workplace, but this is not an integral part of the tech-prep model.

Success of current efforts to build a new school-to-work transition system will depend on whether a sufficient number of employers are willing to make high-quality work-based learning available to high school students. Given the general scarcity of career jobs in the US labor market, there are grounds for skepticism (Bailey, 1993). Finding enough well-designed training placements will be a major challenge for the new school-to-work initiatives.

A second major strategic element of school-to-work programs is combining the academic and vocational curriculum. This is believed to offer more effective instruction for a broad range of students. Potentially it can improve students' learning in academic subjects by placing it in a practical context that gives concrete meaning to theories and abstract information (Resnick, 1987a and 1987b; Raizen, 1989; Berryman and Bailey, 1992). At the same time, it can deepen the intellectual content of vocational subjects.

The question of whether to integrate or separate high school academic and vocational courses has been hotly disputed during most of this century (Lazerson and Grubb, 1974), as the high school evolved from an elite institution to a comprehensive one. The traditional academic curriculum did not seem relevant or appealing to students who were likely to go to work full time after leaving high school. On the other hand, John Dewey and others argued that a vocational curriculum created especially for non-college-bound students might limit their learning unnecessarily. In spite of that risk, the 1917 Smith-Hughes Act began to provide federal support for vocational education, and separate programs were created.

Employers generally supported vocational education when it started and up until the 1980s. Then, in an important shift, some business leaders began to express concern that vocational programs were not giving students sufficient intellectual preparation for the emerging learning-intensive workplace (National Academy of Sciences, 1984; Committee for Economic Development, 1985; Kearns and Doyle, 1988). Evaluations of secondary vocational programs also failed to find that they helped most participating students get jobs; that research is reviewed in Chapter 4. The upshot was that, in the 1990 amendments to the Carl D. Perkins Vocational and Applied Technology Education Act, Congress restricted the federal basic grant for vocational education to be spent only on programs that integrate academic and vocational education.

Combined academic and vocational curriculum is a defining characteristic of career academies. It is also usually present in tech-prep and youth apprenticeship. These and other programs that include an integrated academic/vocational curriculum are reviewed in Chapter 4. Some school-based enterprises apply and develop ideas from both academic and vocational subjects, but most have been tied to vocational classes.

Similarly, at the secondary level co-op usually has been reserved for vocational students.

Although some programs that include a combined vocational/academic curriculum have received positive evaluations, and many schools are making efforts in this direction, this element of school-to-work reform also represents a major challenge. Some degree of integration can be achieved relatively easily, but creating a coherent curriculum that ties together several courses over a period of several years is a large task.

A third major common element of school-to-work programs is explicit linkage between high school and post-secondary studies. This provides access to careers requiring higher education, and prevents the school-to-work program from being stigmatized as an option only for students who lack the ability or ambition to attend college. Secondary-post-secondary linkage is a defining feature of tech-prep, and is also emphasized in youth apprenticeship. Although the majority of career academy graduates go on to two- or four-year colleges, there are not usually any explicit articulation agreements. Co-op and school-based enterprise at the secondary level have tended not to be college-oriented because they have been tied to a traditional vocational curriculum.

In contrast to the widespread agreement among school-to-work program advocates on the goals of integrating work-based with school-based learning and combining vocational with academic curriculum content, there is some disagreement about whether linking high school with post-secondary education should mean ensuring access to four-year institutions, or only to two-year college (Rosenbaum, 1992). Among high school students themselves, half or more aspire to attend a four-year college or university. Although Secretary of Labor Robert Reich and others correctly point out that '75 per cent of young Americans . . . don't graduate from college' (Reich, 1993), it is also true that 63 per cent of the high school graduating class of 1992 went directly to colleges or universities (US Department of Labor, 1993c). This was 'an all-time high'. Of those new high school graduates attending college in October, 1992, 63 per cent (coincidentally) were starting four-year programs. Since a large proportion of those enrolling in two-year programs also intend to transfer to four-year institutions, the total proportion of new high school graduates who are going right to college with the intent of obtaining a bachelor's degree is about 50 per cent. Many of these do not achieve their goal, but the goal is at least strong enough to get them started.

One reason why so many high school students want bachelor's degrees is the monetary payoff, which also recently reached an all-time high (Katz and Murphy, 1992; Levy and Murnane, 1992). The additional earnings associated with a bachelor's degree are much greater than with a two-year associate degree. For instance, Grubb (1993a) analyzed annual earnings of male graduates from the National Longitudinal Study of the High School Class of 1972. Earnings were reported for 1985, thirteen years after graduation. The regression analysis controlled for family background, high school grades, and work experience. A bachelor's degree was associated with additional earnings of $2957 for salaried workers, and $11,541 for self-employed individuals. An associate degree in a vocational field was correlated with additional earnings of only $358 for salaried workers, and self-employed workers with vocational associate degrees actually earned $3076 less, holding other variables constant. An associate degree in an academic field was also correlated with lower earnings: a reduction of $1875 for salaried workers and $3500 for the self-employed. None of the differences in earnings correlated with associate degrees was statistically significant when work experience was statistically held constant.

This makes it important to consider whether linking secondary and post-secondary education means that new school-to-work opportunities will lead to two-year, or also to four-year colleges. Tech-prep programs authorized by the 1990 Perkins Amendments encompass the last two years of high school and the first two years of college, creating a '2 + 2' sequence. These are tailor-made for two-year colleges offering vocational courses. Although four-year institutions are also eligible to participate, either by themselves in a '2 + 4' sequence or with a two-year college in a '2 + 2 + 2' plan, most tech-prep programs in fact are linking high schools with two-year colleges only. Many new youth apprenticeship programs are also combining work-based learning with a tech-prep 2 + 2 curriculum leading from high school to a two-year college.

Programs linking high schools with two-year, not four-year, colleges are unlikely to attract high school students who want bachelor's degrees. That is a problem, not only because the number of students who want bachelor's degrees is large, but more importantly because students who want bachelor's degrees are in some ways more ambitious and are more likely to perform well academically. If these students reject school-to-work programs, the new programs could acquire a second-rate image. This has been a problem with traditional vocational education. A bad image can make it difficult also to attract good teachers, and may make employers reluctant to provide training placements on which the programs depend. In the worst case, the programs could come to be seen as another kind of dumping ground for the non-academically inclined, where poor performance and low expectations would reinforce each other.

Discussion of these strategic questions will be taken up again in Chapter 4. The next four chapters present what is known about school-to-work programs in actual practice.

2 School-and-Work Programs in Secondary Schools

In this chapter we examine school-to-work programs that are widespread in US high schools and secondary vocational centers. Of these, cooperative education is the most common and most established. More recent, but rapidly spreading, are various forms of new youth apprenticeship. Another traditional, but often overlooked, approach is school-based enterprise. In addition to these three forms of school-supervised work experience, we also discuss the effects of other work experience and non-school-supervised jobs, which most students now hold at some time during high school.

Cooperative Education

The 1990 Carl Perkins Act defined cooperative education as:

> a method of instruction of vocational education for individuals who, through written cooperative arrangements between the school and employers, receive instruction, including required academic courses and related vocational instruction by alternation of study in school with a job in any occupational field. Such alternation shall be planned and supervised by the school and employers so that each contributes to the student's education and to his or her employability. Work periods and school attendance may be on alternative half days, full days, weeks, or other periods of time in fulfilling the cooperative program.

Cooperative education has been recognized by federal authority since the regulations implementing the 1917 Smith-Hughes Act. In the 1960s and 1970s federal vocational education statutes provided specific categorical support for cooperative education, but current law no longer does. In fact, although the 1990 Perkins Act continues to define cooperative education, it is otherwise virtually silent on the subject, mentioning it in passing only twice (sections 365(2)(B) and 404(b)(2)). In comparison, apprenticeship, which enrolls far fewer students, is mentioned at least six times. The venerable co-op method seems almost to be taken for granted.

The lack of attention to cooperative education in the latest federal law on vocational education is symptomatic. Until quite recently, when there has been some renewed interest, cooperative education has been virtually absent from policy discussions about preparing the workforce. During the 1980s it was an idea with no cachet.

Lack of interest has also meant lack of evaluation, especially for cooperative education in high schools. The Higher Education Act has provided funds for research and evaluation of cooperative education in post-secondary institutions, but there has been no money earmarked for the secondary level. As a result, in recent years there have been only one or two significant inquiries into high school cooperative education.

Research Findings

Research before 1990 was reviewed by Stern, McMillion, Hopkins and Stone (1990). For convenience, that review will be briefly recapitulated here. One of the most thorough studies was by Herrnstadt, Horowitz and Sum (1979). They interviewed 427 male seniors in cooperative vocational education, regular vocational education, work-study, and the 'general academic' program in a north-eastern metropolitan high school. The sample was resurveyed three times, the last time between seventeen and twenty-one months after graduation. The researchers described their findings as 'mixed'. Co-op students did not experience higher rates of labor force participation, employment, or wages. On the other hand, co-op students were more likely to value the jobs they held in high school, receive on-the-job training from their employers while in high school, claim that their high school programs favorably affected their decision to stay in school, attend classes during senior year, obtain a full-time job immediately following graduation, obtain a job related to their high school program, and express more satisfaction with their final jobs. In short, co-op students were more positive about school and its relationship to employment, but they were no more successful than other students in finding work or earning high wages.

A similar pattern of results emerged from a large, federally sponsored, longitudinal evaluation of several programs that combined school and work, including cooperative vocational education (Walsh and Breglio, 1976). Co-op students were more likely to say that their satisfaction with school had improved after taking their jobs, and that these jobs fit with their career interests. However, in the post-school follow-up two years later, students who had participated in school-supervised employment, including co-op, were less likely to be employed and more likely to be looking for work. Among those who were working, the ones who had been in school-supervised jobs two years earlier usually did report higher earnings, though.

Analysis of the three major national longitudinal surveys has usually failed to find positive economic outcomes for high school co-op students. Lewis, Gardner and Seitz (1983) looked at early (through 1980) follow-up data from the National Longitudinal Survey of Youth Labor Market Experience (NLSY), which started in 1979 with individuals aged 14 to 21. They found no higher earnings or lower unemployment during the first few years after high school for former students who had been in school-supervised jobs — which included co-op, work-study, or in-school programs sponsored by the Comprehensive Employment and Training Act of 1973 (CETA). Bishop, Blakemore and Low (1985) analyzed October 1973 data from the National Longitudinal Study of the High School Class of 1972 (NLS72), and spring 1982 data from 1980 seniors in the High School and Beyond (HSB) survey. They found participation in co-op or work-study was positively related to post-school wages and fraction of time employed in the NLS72 data, but the opposite was true for the HSB sample.

To summarize, this review found evidence that participation in co-op was associated with more positive attitudes toward school and a stronger perceived connection between school and work, but no consistent association between participation in co-op and subsequent success in the labor market. A review of other studies by Leske and Persico (1984) reached the same conclusions. Taken at face value, these results seem to imply that creating a stronger connection between school and work for high school students does not improve their prospects in the labor market after high school. They raise a clear warning flag for proponents of current efforts to expand school-to-work programs.

One possible reason why co-op students apparently do not obtain any significant advantage in the labor market in the first few years after high school is that they do not receive any formal certification that is recognized by other employers. Any gain in knowledge, skill, or work habits resulting from the co-op experience may fail to pay off in the short run if former co-op students do not keep working for their co-op employer, because other employers cannot readily recognize these gains.

Therefore, if they are not given a permanent job by their co-op employer, the former co-op student may have no particular advantage over other former students in the labor market. This possible explanation can be tested by comparing the labor market experience of former students who do and do not obtain permanent jobs with their high school employers. In a test using Colorado data, Stern and Stevens (1992) found that former co-op students who kept working for their co-op employers did experience significantly higher earnings than other former students who also continued working for their high school employers, while among students who changed employers former co-op students had no advantage.

It is also possible that existing studies have underestimated the effects of co-op participation on labor market outcomes. Methodologically, the studies summarized above shared certain strengths and weaknesses. Strong points were the use of longitudinal data, and multivariate analysis which controlled for measured characteristics of students in trying to estimate the separate effect of participation in co-op. One weak point was that most of these studies lumped together co-op and other school-supervised work experience programs, despite the fact that co-op has a relatively rigorous format, as described below. They also merged specialized co-op, in which the teacher in a particular field supervises only students working in that field, with diversified co-op, where students working in various fields are supervised by a coordinator who does not necessarily teach in any of those fields. Another weakness has been failure to correct for possible bias associated with unobserved variables that may affect the probability of participation in co-op.

In addition, an important limitation of these studies has been their failure to account for variation in the quality of students' jobs. The implicit assumption has been that differences among co-op jobs are negligible compared to the difference between co-op and non-co-op jobs. This seems unlikely. Even in well-run co-op programs, some placements offer more complexity, autonomy and opportunity to learn than other placements do. Ignoring this variation may make it more difficult to tell whether being in co-op makes a difference. It also makes it more difficult to explain why co-op makes a difference, if it does.

A recent study by Stone, Stern, Hopkins and McMillion (1990) was designed to measure qualitative characteristics of students' jobs. On average, co-op students are more likely than classmates employed in non-co-op jobs to report that their work provides opportunities to learn a variety of new things, that they use reading and writing on the job in addition to other things they have learned in school, that they have contact with adults on the job and good relationships with their supervisors, that the job is related to their desired career, and that the work is meaningful and motivating. Notwithstanding these average differences, there are still some non-co-op students who describe their jobs more favorably than co-op students do. It should therefore be possible to test whether or not co-op participation has an effect on students' subsequent performance, separately from whether or not it affects the quality of students' work experience while they are in school.

Two other recent studies also should be mentioned. One is a short-term longitudinal study conducted by the New York State Department of Education (1990). Secondary students who had completed occupational education programs offered by school districts or BOCES (Boards of Cooperative Educational Services, providers of various specialized programs including occupational education) were surveyed approximately six months after leaving high school. Comparing co-op to non-co-op students, the survey found co-op students were more likely to report working as their primary activity (53 per cent versus 40 per cent), but less likely to report post-secondary education (36 versus 47 per cent).

A similar pattern was discovered by the US General Accounting Office (1991), which reanalyzed 1982 data from the 1980 HSB seniors. Among co-op participants, 74 per cent reported they were working for pay (not necessarily their primary activity), compared to 57 per cent of all seniors in fall, 1981. But only 33 per cent of former co-op students were in some kind of post-secondary education (25 per cent in two- or four-year college and 8 per cent in vocational or technical schools), compared to 53 per cent of all seniors (46 per cent in colleges and 7 per cent in vocational or technical schools). This is consistent with the fact that a large proportion of co-op students, while they were still in high school, identified themselves as being in the vocational track. Compared to other seniors, co-op students also came from lower socio-economic backgrounds and had lower scores on the HSB test of vocabulary, reading and math.

These two studies reflect the fact that co-op programs in high school have been tied to vocational education, and have not been seen as part of the college-prep curriculum, though they have kept the college option open for some students. However, lacking statistical controls for other characteristics of students, these two studies were not designed to measure the extent to which co-op adds to, or detracts from, students' subsequent success in school or work.

The GAO study does signal a rekindling of interest in co-op among policy makers. The study estimated how many high school students currently participate in co-op. As of 1989/90, a survey of state directors of cooperative education yielded an estimate of 'about 430,000' students nationwide. This was less than 4 per cent of total high school enrollment, but it represents about 8 per cent of the juniors and seniors, who comprise most of the co-op participants. These estimates correspond closely to findings from the 1992 NAVE survey of secondary schools, which estimated that co-op enrollment in 1990/91 represented 3.7 per cent of all students in grades 9–12, or 7.7 per cent of juniors and seniors (Stern, 1992a). The NAVE survey further indicates that another 1.8 per cent of students in grades 9–12, or 3.7 per cent of juniors and seniors, were participating in other school-based work experience programs which often possess the characteristics of co-op (see table 2 below). It would therefore be accurate to say that approximately 5 per cent of students in grades 9–12, or 10 per cent of seniors, were in programs which were either called co-op or had all the main features of co-op.

The GAO study also included a review of practices in eleven high school sites (and eight community colleges) chosen from a list of programs recommended by co-op researchers and practitioners. Based on these site visits, GAO concluded that well-run co-op programs apparently help students both in finding permanent jobs and in preparing for further education. Employers apparently benefit from the extra motivation of co-op students and also from the chance to 'try out' possible permanent employees. Schools reportedly gain from increased student interest and connections with employers.

Certain problems also were mentioned in the GAO study. One is the 'negative reputation that many people have of co-op programs and vocational education in general' (p. 34). This contributes to reluctance of non-vocational teachers to recommend students for co-op. It also repels parents who fear that co-op will detract from their children's chances of attending college. The challenge here is to make co-op part of the integration of academic and vocational education that is envisioned by the Perkins Act.

GAO also emphasized the lack of uniform certification for co-op completers. Co-op is like a short-term apprenticeship but, unlike traditional apprenticeship, it does not result in any kind of skill certification that is recognized by employers at large. Current national efforts to create skill standards for specific occupations and industries should help provide a target for which co-op programs can aim. Common skill standards might facilitate employment of co-op graduates who do not find permanent jobs with their co-op employers. As suggested above, this might resolve in practice the puzzle revealed by research: that co-op succeeds in creating a strong connection between school and work, but former co-op students generally do not obtain any significant advantage in employment or earnings in the first few years after high school.

Elements of Good Practice

The GAO described what it considered to be the elements of a 'high quality' co-op program, based on observations and interviews at the selected program sites. This wisdom of practice has emerged from decades of experience, and has also been articulated elsewhere (National Child Labor Committee, 1984; Leske and Persico, 1984). We offer a brief distillation here (cf. Goldberger, Kazis and O'Flanagan, 1994):

- A written *training agreement* between the school and each employer sets forth the expectations for each party. The employer will provide a job with opportunities to learn. The school will monitor students' performance.
- A written *training plan* for each student is at the heart of the co-op program. It specifies what the student is expected to learn on the job. Learning objectives may be linked to vocational or academic courses. The plan also specifies who will judge whether the student has achieved the stated objectives. It is usually signed by the student, the job supervisor, the co-op coordinator, and sometimes by a parent.
- The co-op *coordinator* may be the teacher in a related class (for example, business or marketing) with responsibility for supervising students only in that field. Alternatively, in a diversified co-op program the coordinator supervises students from several fields. The coordinator also may have special training and certification as a co-op specialist. The coordinator's responsibilities include:

  — Finding suitable job placements. Some programs provide summer salary for co-ordinators to come back early for this purpose. In well established programs, employers initiate placements by calling the school and requesting a co-op student. It is considered desirable for the coordinator to visit the worksite before placing a student there, to make sure the employer understands the responsibility entailed in hiring a co-op student. The training agreement embodies this understanding.

— Identifying suitable students for each placement. It is considered advisable to refer more than one student for the employer to interview. This gives students practice in job interviews, and gives the employer some choice.
— Negotiating training plans for all students.
— Monitoring students on the job. Coordinators must have released time during the day for this purpose. By visiting the job site, the coordinator can ensure that both the student and the job supervisor are satisfied with the way things are going. If there are problems, the coordinator can try to mediate or, if that fails, can remove the student from the job. At the end of the student's placement, the coordinator is responsible, usually in collaboration with the job supervisor, for evaluating students' performance according to their training plans.
— Offering related instruction. If the co-op program is offered in conjunction with a regular class, the coordinator would normally be the teacher in that class, which would naturally deal with issues from students' jobs. In a diversified program there may be a special class for co-op students, which would deal with more generic issues about work.

Data on the actual prevalence of some of these characteristics are available from the National Assessment of Vocational Education (NAVE) survey of high schools and secondary vocational centers (Stern, 1992a). Table 2 shows the weighted percentages of schools indicating that their co-op programs had the specified features. The large majority of responses are affirmative, except that in only about half the co-op programs do the coordinators find jobs for students and have some paid time during the summer for that purpose. These exceptions point to the fact that paying school staff to find jobs for students is expensive — but this is an expense that will have to be incurred by any school-to-work program that does not rely on students to find their own jobs.

Also shown in table 2 are the percentages of schools indicating that this same list of features are present in two types of work experience program that are similar to co-op. One is in-field work experience (IFWE), defined in the survey as a program that does 'not qualify as cooperative education but allows students to earn school credit in conjunction with paid or unpaid employment in their vocational field of study'. The second is other work experience (OWE), which 'allows students to earn school credit in conjunction with paid or unpaid employment outside their vocational field of study'. Schools indicate

Table 2: Weighted percentage* of secondary schools reporting specified features of school-to-work programs

	Co-op	IFWE	OWE
Written training plan required for each student	92.0	85.4	74.4
Content of training plan includes:			
Reading and writing	80.3	74.6	71.8
Arithmetic or other mathematics	79.5	73.5	66.9
Listening and speaking	86.4	80.0	79.8
Creative thinking and problem solving	83.6	75.8	76.3
Organizing time and other resources	88.6	83.6	75.8
Acquiring and using information	87.2	84.5	82.5
Coordinators supervise in own subject only	71.4	65.7	42.0
Coordinators, not students themselves, find jobs	56.9	53.5	54.0
Coordinators meet employer before student is placed	83.0	79.9	70.5
Coordinators have release time to visit job sites	94.6	85.3	82.3
Coordinators are paid at least one month in summer	46.7	38.2	34.1
Limit on the number of students per coordinator	71.3	67.8	59.1
Students absent from school are prohibited from working that day	78.8	73.4	70.5
Employers provide assurances of opportunities for students to learn on the job	97.1	93.7	87.5
Employers provide assurances of ability to provide supervision	97.9	96.8	91.4
Employers' evaluation influence students' grades	96.5	92.8	89.9
To be eligible, students must complete a separate course of related instruction	72.1	58.7	44.9
To be eligible, students must have a grade-point average above a specified minimum	35.5	35.9	25.9

* Only schools that reported presence of each program are included.

that both of these programs usually share the defining feature of co-op, though to a somewhat lesser extent. The biggest differences are in whether students are required to complete a separate course of related instruction, and whether coordinators supervise only in their own field of specialization — co-op programs more often possess both of these features. However, the fact that many of these other school-supervised work experience programs do share the features of co-op means that, in effect, there are students who participate in co-op even though they use another name for it.

Youth Apprenticeship

In this section we describe recent attempts to revitalize the apprenticeship concept by using it to bridge the gap between high school, post-secondary education, and work. We discuss definitions of youth apprenticeship, assess the responsibilities of the parties involved, and raise the issue of balance between the goals of job preparation and academic upgrading. Individual programs, while similar in overall objectives, are unique as they account for career focus, budget limitations and institutional partnerships. To make the discussion more concrete, we describe five ongoing projects. Two of these are local pilot programs and three of these are directed and organized at the state level.

Our description of one of the pilot studies — Project ProTech in Boston — includes a first-year formative evaluation. This points out the kinds of opportunities and hurdles these programs may face as they develop. Most of the other youth apprenticeship efforts are too new to have been formally evaluated, so we report instead the views and opinions of individuals responsible for the efforts.

Defining Youth Apprenticeship

The definition of youth apprenticeship in the US is still evolving. Some definitions deal with overall goals and vague aims of youth apprenticeship, while others are more detailed. Among the latter there is variation in the relative importance of work and school, and the role of key participants.

The essential idea of youth apprenticeship is to provide structured, work-based learning for high school students, who are too young and too numerous to qualify for the small number of formal, registered apprenticeship programs that exist in the US. This is consistent with the School-to-Work Opportunities Act of 1994 that aims to catalyze the development of a school-to-work system in this country. Writing for Jobs for the Future, the leading organization in the development of youth apprenticeship for the US, Roditi (1991) explains the concept of youth apprenticeship as:

> apprenticeship because at the heart of these systems is the integration of school and workplace learning and an emphasis on learning-by-doing under the tutelage of experts; and youth, because these systems address the personal and professional development of young people. (p. 3)

Jobs for the Future has indicated the need to provide institutional supports for these programs that go beyond 'program' elements. A system of work-based learning in the United States, instead, depends on transferable credentials in occupation-specific areas (Bailey and Merritt, 1993; Rosenbaum, 1992). Further, Hamilton noted that a nationwide system to support youth apprenticeships would have to include

'(1) a legal definition and basis; (2) institutional supports in the public and private sectors that reduce coordination, design, and implementation challenges; (3) curricula for school and work based learning; and (4) incentives for participation from key groups, particularly employers' (JFF, 1993a).

The most important elements of youth apprenticeship are summarized by Jobs for the Future (*ibid*) as follows:

- Employers provide paid work experience and guided worksite learning.
- Schools integrate academic and vocational learning.
- School and workplace learning are coordinated and integrated.
- Programs articulate high school and post-secondary learning and are at least two years in duration.
- Completers receive widely recognized credentials of both academic and occupational skill mastery.
- Programs are governed by broad coalitions of institutional partners.

This concept of youth apprenticeship importantly includes preparation for post-secondary education as well as for work. Kazis and Roche (1991), for example, view youth apprenticeship as an extension of the tech-prep model that includes work-based learning opportunities. In contrast, earlier school-to-apprenticeship models were designed to prepare students to enter formal, registered apprenticeships.

Another proponent of the broad conception of youth apprenticeship is Nothdurft (1990), who outlines potential benefits for each key participant. For young students, it provides early exposure to the world of work, an opportunity to 'broaden the base of their education in applied settings and mature gradually in the company of adults who care about them' (p. 13). Employers are expected to benefit from having an impact on building a quality workforce. Schools have an opportunity to bridge the world of work and the world of school which in turn will 'enliven the educational process, invigorate teachers and make students eager learners' (p. 14). Finally, communities should benefit from having more responsible citizens as manifested by less street crime, fewer dropouts, and less drug abuse. In its Employer's Guide to Youth Apprenticeship, the National Alliance of Business (1992) provides a similarly broad list of anticipated benefits of youth apprenticeship programs for students, employers, school and communities (p. 13), as well as a list of various roles each of these participants will play in the process (p. 24).

Hoyt (1991) identifies three distinct 'proposals' for youth apprenticeship. The first proposal refers to the application of the apprenticeship concept in entry-level training for traditionally non-apprenticeship occupations. It has been promoted by USDOL's Office of Work-Based Learning. The second proposal is grounded in Hamilton's *Apprenticeship for Adulthood* (1990), which calls for a comprehensive educational system. The backbone is a 2-plus-2 program combining the last two years of high school and the first two years of college with highly structured work experience. Finally, Hoyt recognizes Lerman and Pouncy's (1990) view as a third proposal, calling for formal contracts between eleventh graders and specific employers. The program would last three years, and time spent in on-the-job activities would gradually increase, up to at least 75 per cent in the last year.

Roditi (1991) also describes three alternative models of youth apprenticeship, classified by degree of independence from the high school. Roditi refers to the first model as the independent teacher team, in which fifty to 100 students are assigned to a team of three to five teachers, as a self-contained unit. Teachers plan the curriculum and regularly visit students' workplaces. Teaching can occur inside or outside the high school. An example of this model is LaGuardia Middle College High School, where students get thirteen weeks unpaid work experience each year in high school. One feature of the Pennsylvania Youth Apprenticeship Program (see appendix A) is that an increasing portion of students' time is spent at the workplace over the course of four years.

Roditi's second model is a partially independent teacher team where: (1) participating students take some special classes together, and some with regular high school students and teachers; (2) some teachers might teach both regular high school students and youth apprentices; (3) the team has a limited administrative independence; and (4) the team is school-based (p. 16). Career academies like the Oakland Media Academy exemplify this model. Roditi suggests that the Fort Wayne Youth Apprenticeship program is expected to apply the principles of this model.

The third model is the one with no independent teacher team. Here (1) apprentices take most or all of their classes with regular high school students and teachers; (2) all participating teachers teach both high school students and youth apprentices; (3) the participating teachers have almost no administrative independence; and (4) the program is school-based. Tech-prep programs are an example of this model. In the Tech Prep Associate Degree Health Occupations Project, students in Paris, Texas, spend six hours a week in four-week hospital rotations. Some related curriculum is provided. Also representing this model is the Portland Partnership Project, where students work in the afternoons and during summers.

Description of Youth Apprenticeship Initiatives

Youth apprenticeship sites in 1993 were sponsored by the Department of Labor through demonstration grants (ten sites), by Jobs for the Future (six sites), some jointly (four sites), and others independently (thirty-four sites). Several states have recently initiated efforts to expand youth apprenticeship programs. While it is estimated that a few thousand students are currently enrolled, support through the proposed School to Work Opportunities Act is likely to result in enrollment increases in these programs. Many of these new programs will focus on the health care, machining, electronics, and hospitality industries. (Finkelstein and Latting, forthcoming).

In general, programs have targeted industries, employer contacts, and a plan for their students' course of training. They vary over a wide range of concentrations from aerospace (Middle Georgia Technical Institute, Warner Robins, GA) to metalworking (Craftsmanship 2000, Tulsa, OK), to health careers (Health Occupations Program, Kalamazoo, MI). McDonald's Youth Apprenticeship Program is in the planning stages in Indianapolis, Chicago, and Detroit as a four-year business management program with specialization in food service management. States are also capitalizing on momentum in this field. The California New Youth Apprenticeship Project (CNYAP) is a consortium of three programs in graphic arts, health and construction in separate locations. While most of the programs are serving small numbers of students (twelve to fifty annually), a few of the programs have plans in place for several hundred students annually. The descriptions that follow illustrate the variation in programs. The first example, that of Project ProTech in Boston, has been formally evaluated after year one and allows for some consideration of the relevant planning and implementation issues.

Project ProTech, Boston Massachusetts. Project ProTech began in the fall of 1991 as a youth apprenticeship program in allied health careers. The program combines classroom learning from four high schools, clinical experiences in Boston's hospitals, and continuation to include at least two years of post-secondary education. The objective of the program is to train students who are thought to be non-college-bound in areas of high skill in health-related fields. Further, the sponsors hope to enrich the instruction of high school courses to make them relevant in career development.

The formative evaluation of Project ProTech provided by Jobs For the Future (Goldberger, 1993) summarizes the findings from the first year in six areas: the partnership; learning through work; integrating school and work; unifying high school and post-secondary training; student selection and outcomes; and achieving a cost-effective design.

The first year of Project ProTech has demonstrated the complexity of the institutional partnerships that support the program. In this case the Boston Private Industry Council (PIC) was valuable in representing the hospitals as a unified group. At the same time, the PIC was less successful as a broker between the hospitals and the schools. It was recommended that additional attention be paid to representing the schools and hospitals as equal partners in the ongoing development of ProTech as significant flexibility is required from both groups to accommodate the program's needs.

Clinical instruction was widely used to support the curriculum in Project ProTech. This has evolved over the first year as the most effective instruction provided by the hospital was in rotations through departments as on-the-job training. While the work-based component was generally successful, the quality of job placements varied. Good clinical instruction required a combination of supervision, support, the development of a learning plan and training for hospital staff.

The integration of academic and vocational curriculum was limited during the first year. Most of the recommendations called for curriculum and staff development to take advantage of a school-based curriculum that focuses on applications learned in the workplace. Teachers need greater understanding of the students' hospital experience to develop curriculum that is current and consistent. Changing scheduling at the school-site and promoting the program among other teachers were reported as other areas for improvement.

Project ProTech by design includes a post-secondary component that continues the secondary model. It is important that the transition be seamless from high school to college which includes an entire new set of partnerships and curriculum alignment. At the end of the first year, these issues had not been worked out with post-secondary institutions.

The performance of students in Project ProTech varied considerably during the first year. Those students who did participate all year and had quality job placements appeared to develop greater confidence and showed increased motivation to perform on the job. Those students who entered with poor academic histories continued to have trouble with this program design. As a result, program designers concluded this model would not be accessible to students with severe academic and behavioral problems. Further, this led to the conclusion that nearly half of the high school students in Boston would be unable to participate in a program of this kind.

Finally, the cost of ProTech in the first year was $450,000 and reached eighty-eight students initially, fifty-four of whom stayed in the program the entire year. Costs incurred directly by the hospitals are not included. Project researchers concluded that costs will need to be evaluated for the program to be continued as part of a mainstream model of career education. Central staff were added to help in the development of the program in the first year. Streamlining the program by reducing staff or by substituting staff from school personnel could help reduce costs.

Broome County Youth Apprenticeship Demonstration Project, Broome County, New York. Another important youth apprenticeship initiative is in Broome County, New York (see appendix A). This is a pilot project conceived and organized by Stephen and Mary Agnes Hamilton and their colleagues from Cornell University. The project started in the fall of 1991, when twenty-two eleventh graders enrolled in apprenticeships in health care, manufacturing and engineering technology, and administrative and office technology. Apprenticeships were provided by four employers. In the fall of 1992, twenty of these students went on to their second year of the program, and twenty more students were enrolled. Also, an additional two employers provided apprenticeships. The program recruits students whose grade-point average is just above C, and who are not considered at risk of dropping out of high school. After initial screening by school staff students are screened by program staff and steering committee members.

The Hamiltons refer to their model as a work-based tech-prep option. Students spend ten to twenty hours per week at work. Most of the work is done in the after-school hours, and full-time during summers. In this respect, the project resembles a traditional cooperative vocational education program, except that work is more carefully planned than in most actual co-op programs, and the high school experience is formally linked with post-secondary education. In school, teachers and counselors provide a forum for discussing work related issues. In 1992/93 special projects were added to the program. These are extended academic activities in which the youth apprentice explores in depth an issue of importance at work.

The Broome County project is competency based. It is intended to include performance based assessments rather than seat time as the evaluation base of the apprentices. The list of key competencies expected to be developed and evaluated at the workplace includes: using proper procedures to accomplish a task, using computer technology, following rules, understanding principles and procedures, understanding organizational systems, communicating, working in teams, taking responsibility, and committing to excellence. The list is adapted to each apprentice.

The relationship with community colleges is still not clearly defined, as the project has not yet reached that stage of development. The employers have committed to four years of participation. Students are paid initially at the minimum wage, and wages are expected to increase each year.

Pennsylvania's Multi-Site Youth Apprenticeship Program. Pennsylvania's initiative came from the State Department of Commerce, and was started in 1991 with a pilot site that enrolled twelve students. This site served for observation and research. Five additional demonstration programs were launched in September 1992. There are presently 350 students participating in sixteen sites across the state. They are placed with 148 employers, mainly small tool and die makers and machinery manufacturers. Recruitment was open to all students.

The criteria for acceptance included recommendations of a guidance counselor, parents' approval and having been hired by a participating employer. Schoolwork requirements vary to meet local needs. Generally, students have classroom instruction on Mondays and Tuesdays, worksite training on Wednesdays and Thursdays, and more classroom instruction on Fridays. Such a design enables adequate communication and feedback. Students are taught by both academic and vocational teachers who are using an expanded and innovative curriculum. The assumption is that the youth apprenticeship curriculum represents an ever-evolving program and therefore needs to adapt continuously to the changing world.

Each student is assigned a mentor and a journeyperson. Students are paid a stipend by the employer. The time spent at the work site will gradually increase during the four years of the program. It is expected that in the second (senior) year of the program the format will be reversed to going to school two days and working three days. Students' progress will be assessed based on demonstrations of competencies. Regional employer groups, formed for the youth apprenticeship program, have taken part in developing training matrices for the work site curriculum. A training matrix covers approximately 5050 hours of training.

State of Wisconsin Youth Apprenticeship Program. Wisconsin's 1991 youth apprenticeship law created a program (see appendix A) and designated the state's Department of Industry, Labor and Human Relations to carry out the related activities in cooperation with the Department of

Public Instruction and the Wisconsin Board of Vocational, Technical and Adult Education. Wisconsin has the oldest registered apprenticeship system in the nation. Much of its youth apprenticeship model is based on elements of the traditional program.

The expected outcomes for the student participants will be: (1) to enter work at a higher rate of pay; (2) to receive an advanced standing in a registered adult apprenticeship (up to one-and-a-half years); (3) to receive an advanced standing in a technical college; and (4) to master a curriculum that meets the admission requirements for the university system.

Implementation of youth apprenticeship began in the fall of 1992 with two programs, both in the printing industry. One site includes one school district and a single employer, with twelve students enrolled. Students spend four hours a day in school and four hours in the work-based learning site. Two days a week, they spend one to one-and-a half hours attending courses at a technical college. Students will work full-time during the summer.

The other Wisconsin site included four school districts in a consortium arrangement with four participating employers. Nine students are enrolled in the program. They will rotate among the four employers. Students take all of their academic and technical courses at a technical college; academic teachers from the high school come to teach at the college. Students spend Mondays and Tuesdays in school, eight hours each day, and the rest of the week at the work site. Such scheduling and location arrangements help solve transportation and coaching problems.

Another printing program was scheduled to start in Milwaukee in 1993 for twenty-five students. Also in 1993, a finance curriculum — to be developed with the help of local banks, savings and loans institutions and credit unions — will be implemented. Other programs in the utilities industry, hospitality industry, and motor vehicle equipment sales are scheduled to start in 1994.

To be eligible for youth apprenticeship, students must pass the tenth grade Gateway Assessment Exam (or a proxy) and complete an approved industry-specific survey course which includes an overview of the technology requirements, occupational options, and wage and employment expectations. The first generation of student participants is taking this course in their first semester of the program. All students are required to enter into a written agreement with their high school, parents and employer. The agreement is approved by the Wisconsin Department of Labor, Industry and Human Relations, which is also responsible for approving agreements in the registered apprenticeship system.

Arkansas Youth Apprenticeship Initiative. In 1991, the state of Arkansas began a youth apprenticeship program with technical assistance from Jobs For the Future. Recruitment of tenth graders started in spring, 1992. Approximately 150 apprenticeships were awarded for fall 1992. The program is expected to include the last two years of high school and the first two years of college. Approximately seventy firms are preparing apprenticeships in health services, industrial machinery maintenance and repair, small retail management, metalworking, and food service production and management. Firms will receive an incentive for cooperation in the form of tax breaks. Particularly good cooperation was established with firms that have their headquarters in Arkansas (for example, Tyson and Wal-Mart). The program is set up to increase movement of apprentices from one employer to another. All apprentices will start at minimum wage with a possibility of advancement. Firms are not explicitly expected to hire apprentices after the end of their training.

Primary responsibility for oversight rests with the Vocational Technical Education Division of the Arkansas Department of Education, in collaboration with the Arkansas Apprenticeship Coordinating Steering Committee. Six consortia, consisting of representatives from secondary, post-secondary institutions, from businesses and industry and from the legislature, have been approved by the Arkansas Department of Education for implementation of youth apprenticeship.

Emerging Issues

This section summarizes the issues that emerged from discussions with individuals directly involved in the development and implementation of the youth apprenticeship concept.[1] One issue is the name, 'youth apprenticeship'. In the minds of many, apprenticeship is not related to academic education and it is difficult to advocate or promote 'apprenticeship' as a possible means of transition to college or university. It has been suggested that youth apprenticeship be developed in relatively attractive, high-prestige occupations which, possibly, would promote a favorable image of the program. Presently, it is difficult to convince parents of high school sophomores that their children will be able to go to college after having participated in an apprenticeship program.

Also important is to take into account (in)flexibility of the high school districts to accommodate the new demands of youth apprenticeship programs. For apprenticeship to succeed, Tift (1992) claims, 'schools will have to change their methods, schedules and assumptions. Few teachers are familiar with local, regional and national job requirements; more flexible schedules need to be adopted to meet students' and employers' needs' (p. 4).

Major concerns on the part of the participating firms are labor issues, child labor laws, hazardous occupations, wages and stipends, incentives for participation, and long-term commitment to participation (Jobs for the Future, 1993a). There is a widespread view that union resistance has been a limiting factor in the implementation of youth apprenticeship programs. The resistance of organized labor stems from concerns that young apprentices will displace older workers or undermine wage levels. It is therefore crucial that labor unions are represented in the process of developing youth apprenticeship programs.

Another issue related to employers is providing the right incentives for their participation. Some states are providing tax credits. However, the appropriateness of this is questionable if the benefits of youth apprenticeship programs accrue mainly to apprentices and employers themselves. Furthermore, there is a history in the US of subsidized training being associated with disadvantaged workers whom employers often consider less desirable.

Child labor laws are of concern to management of the participating firms. It is important that advocates of youth apprenticeship programs do not put participating employers in jeopardy due to careless planning or negligence of state or national laws.

Long-term commitment by employers is vital to youth apprenticeship. However, some industries may not be appropriate for youth apprenticeship because of high turnover at the entry level of employment, and short career ladders. Growing employment demand is also necessary to ensure that businesses will participate in the programs out of self-interest, rather than out of forced commitment.

State-level planning and coordination can help target programs to growing industries. It can also help deal with issues such as worker compensation, union concerns, child labor and portability of credentials. On the other hand, local implementation is required to match particular employers and schools. Youth apprenticeship is therefore evolving as a set of local initiatives within a state and federal framework.

As the preceding review has shown, youth apprenticeship has come to mean different things to different people. These differences can be considered on a continuum with programs that prepare students for registered apprenticeships on one end, and youth apprenticeship as a form of pedagogy at the other. This latter view is expressed by the notion of cognitive apprenticeship (Berryman, 1992). Between these ends of the continuum lie the programs reviewed in this report. Each offers a different balance of specific skill development and general academic development. Closer to the traditional apprenticeship end of the continuum we place the Wisconsin experiment, particularly given the articulation potential with established, registered apprenticeships. Closely following is the Pennsylvania model. Both of these are state models that will address, at the state level, the portability of the credential to be earned. More toward the center of the continuum is the Hamiltons' Broome County demonstration, which combines academic and vocational education with the clear intent of continuing education beyond high school. In a similar location on the continuum are Pro Tech and the Arkansas program. Like Broome County, these efforts seek to incorporate the evolving tech-prep 2 plus 2 program. Also like Broome County, Pro Tech and the various efforts in Arkansas are locally initiated; they will have to face the problem of how portable their credentials will be.

Bailey and Merritt (1993) argue that ultimately a system of work-based learning will need to involve employers more than is currently the case. Further, they recommend long-range planning to develop an appropriate set of institutions and incentive systems to help in the replication of workplace education programs. In their view, youth apprenticeship programs will need to evolve over time to make them more consistent with economic and institutional dynamics in this country. Until that time, current initiatives will help to break down the barriers between education and work and provide useful information on program outcomes.

School-Based Enterprise

Growing interest in school-to-work transition and new models of youth apprenticeship have drawn attention to the existence of school-based enterprises, which engage students in school-based activities that produce goods or services for sale or use to people other than the students involved. In high schools and two-year colleges these activities range from Junior Achievement mini-enterprises to students building houses, running restaurants, managing retail stores, repairing and selling cars, raising crops and livestock, staffing child care centers, publishing books and periodicals, conducting studies of environmental quality or energy conservation, reconstructing local historical landmarks, and engaging in small-scale manufacturing (Stern, Stone, Hopkins, McMillion and Crain, 1994). These activities have most often been associated with vocational education, giving students an opportunity to apply knowledge and skills taught in classes. School-based enterprises in high schools or two-year colleges are analogous to practices at the post-graduate level where law students produce law review journals or doctoral students help run research studies. Teaching hospitals associated with medical schools are school-based enterprises at an advanced level.

As noted above, the 1992 NAVE survey found 19 per cent of secondary schools in the US operating some kind of school-based enterprise (Stern, 1992a). This is in spite of the fact that there has never been any federal initiative to promote such activities. In contrast, in the UK during the 1980s the government provided start-up funds, teacher training, and curriculum materials to promote 'mini-enterprises' in schools (Jamieson, Miller and Watts, 1988; Williamson, 1989), with the result that approximately 40 per cent of government-supported secondary schools in the UK were conducting such activities in the late 1980s and early 1990s. School-based enterprises have also been fostered by national governments in a number of developing countries, partly for the purpose of generating revenues to offset the cost of schools (von Borstel, 1982).

Although a number of American school-based enterprises have been described in the literature, there do not appear to have been any quantitative evaluations of what students have learned from them. For present purposes, therefore, a brief description of a few examples must suffice to illustrate what school-based enterprises do. Other cases are described at greater length in Stern *et al.* (1994).

The Montgomery County Students Construction Trades Foundation in Montgomery County, Maryland is an example of school-based enterprise arising out of vocational education (Stern, 1990). Founded by two vocational education teachers at Rockville High School, the Foundation for more than ten years has built houses and sold them on the open market. In addition to those students who physically built the houses, students specializing in other areas were also involved. Architecture students competed for the final design of the house, and interior design students designed the interiors. Landscaping students designed the landscape, cabinetmaking students built cabinets, food service students prepared a buffet for the open house, journalism students wrote press releases, accounting students kept records and prepared financial reports, and marketing students designed brochures and provided customer service for potential buyers. This award-winning program is a particularly good example of the hundreds of house-building enterprises in high schools around the country.

Another school enterprise rooted in traditional vocational education is The Marketplace, a student-run seasonal retail store located in a shopping mall in Fairfax County, Virginia (Burgess, 1987). After conducting market research to identify unfilled market niches in the mall, marketing students enlisted the help of building trades students to construct a kiosk out of which business began. Meantime, the marketing class organized into merchandising, personnel, management, sales promotion, and financial control departments. Each department performed its respective tasks, and their efforts resulted in a 22 per cent profit. Subsequent years proved to be just as successful, and a commercially constructed store replaced the kiosk. Except for the fact that this project is physically located outside the school, it is similar to student-operated stores in numerous high schools, many of which are affiliated with the Distributive Education Clubs of America (DECA).

Restaurants are another common kind of school-based enterprise connected with vocational education. One program designed to broaden the curricular content of school enterprise beyond vocational subjects was called FEAST, for Food Education And Service Technology. Originally sponsored by the Hotel and Restaurant Foundation of the City College of San Francisco, FEAST delivered a complete curriculum built around the food service industry. (This anticipated the concept of a career academy, described below.) At Kennedy High School in Richmond, California, teachers designed an integrated curriculum including English, math and food services. Students ran a restaurant, the school cafeteria, and an after-school catering club. Stern (1984) asked students to compare their school-based work with their experience in jobs outside of school, and found that the school-based enterprises gave students 'more opportunity to work in teams, to learn skills they think will be valuable in future jobs, and to experience work that is more intrinsically motivating' (p. 422).

While most school-based enterprises have grown out of vocational education, there are some that have emerged from the academic side. Probably the most famous example is Foxfire (Wigginton, 1986; Puckett, 1986). Founded by teacher Eliot Wigginton in an attempt to motivate his English students and make the curriculum more relevant to them, Foxfire began with the production of a magazine about local history and culture, which was sold to the community at large. The magazine was so successful that it led to publication of a series of books and production of a play by Foxfire, Inc. Profits have been used to support a network of curriculum and teacher development in the Foxfire method.

Mt. Edgecumbe High School in Sitka, Alaska has also developed an enterprise related to the academic curriculum (Knapp, 1989). In keeping with the school's focus on Pacific Rim studies, Edgecumbe Enterprises involved students in manufacturing smoked fish and marketing it to Pacific Rim countries. Students and teachers made several trips to Japan to analyze the Japanese market first-hand.

Oregon's Sandy Union High School began a program with the specific objective of integrating science and vocational education (Crow *et al.*, 1987), in addition to promoting local environmental improvement. Taking advantage of a forty acre woodland nature preserve next to the school, students designed and built a trail system, improved a stream habitat, and made hatching boxes and fish runs. Environmental action projects like this exist in many schools. Although they may not usually be labeled as school-based enterprise, they clearly do engage students in productive activities from which other people benefit.

REAL Enterprise (1989; Baker, 1990) is an organization that carries the idea of local community development several steps further. REAL helps schools become seedbeds for small enterprises started by students, which they then continue as self-employment after they graduate.

In the context of current efforts to improve the school-to-work transition system in the US, school-based enterprises represent an alternative to non-school enterprises as a location for work-based learning. Bailey and Merritt point out that 'SBE has the advantage of avoiding the need to recruit and retain employer participants' (p. 50). Since schools create these enterprises mainly for educational purposes, they may also be more hospitable than non-school enterprises to activities that are conducive to students' acquisition of knowledge and skill — for example, job rotation, learning from mistakes, and exposure to all aspects of the enterprise. Expansion of school enterprise is possible now that the 1994 School to Work Opportunities Act has given the concept its first legislative endorsement.

Non-School-Supervised Work Experience

Hundreds of thousands of high school students participate in cooperative education each year. Perhaps 100,000 engage in some kind of school-based enterprise. As of 1994 there were a few thousand enrolled in new youth apprenticeships (Finkelstein and Latting, forthcoming). But these participants in various forms of school-supervised work experience are vastly outnumbered by the millions of students who hold paid jobs during the school year without any school supervision. As noted earlier, even co-op and other school-supervised work experience programs rely on students to find their own jobs. It is therefore important not to overlook the effects of these do-it-yourself arrangements for school-to-work transition.

The proportion of high school students who hold paid jobs during the school year has been increasing since the late 1940s, especially for females (Greenberger and Steinberg, 1986; Barton, 1989). The proportion declines during recessions, but the overall trend has been upward. High School and Beyond survey data showed 59 per cent of sophomores and 76 per cent of seniors in 1980 were in the labor force. In the National Longitudinal Survey of Youth data for 1979 to 1981, 64 per cent of high school juniors worked at least one week during the academic year (excluding summer), and 73 per cent of seniors (Ruhm, 1993).

Research evidence generally indicates short-term gains in earnings and access to employment after leaving school, for students who work while in school. However, the evidence also suggests that working long hours while in school may also interfere with educational attainment and thus detract from earnings and occupational status in the long run. As the number of hours per week spent working while in school increases, a trade-off between short-term and long-term economic gains emerges.

Association Between Working While in High School and Employment Outcomes a Few Years Later

All studies have found a positive association between amount of high school work experience and employment or earnings a few years later. The National Longitudinal Survey of the High School Class of 1972 (NLS72) data were analyzed by Meyer and Wise (1982). The National Longitudinal Survey of Youth Labor Market Experience (NLSY) has been analyzed by D'Amico (1984), Stern and Nakata (1989), Steel (1991) and Ruhm (1993). The High School and Beyond survey (HSB) was studied by Bishop, Blakemore and Low (1985) and by Marsh (1991). Mortimer and Finch (1986) analyzed the Youth in Transition Survey (YIT), which followed male sophomores for several years after high school. Meyer and Wise, Stern and Nakata both limited their samples to those not attending college; Ruhm's analysis found this restriction did not make much difference. Steel stratified by race/ethnicity and found positive effect significant only for whites, not blacks or Hispanics.

There is some evidence that jobs which provide greater opportunity for students to use and develop their skills have more positive effects. Analyzing extensive NLSY 1979 data on qualitative characteristics of students' jobs, Stern and Nakata found opportunity for skill use and development was the only qualitative factor that significantly predicted subsequent employment and wages in 1980–82. Mortimer, Ryu, Dennehy and Lee (1992), studying a sample of 1000 randomly chosen ninth graders from St. Paul who were followed to grade 12, examined the relationship between work experience and the development of occupational values. They found no significant effects of hours worked or employment itself on occupational values. However, the opportunity to acquire skills at work had a substantial positive effect on development of intrinsic orientation toward work, that is, interest in rewards embedded in the work activity itself. Similarly, Stern, Stone, Hopkins and McMillion (1990) found in cross-sectional data that students who report greater opportunities for learning on the job also express a more positive orientation toward work in general. The absence of opportunities for skill use and development in jobs held by a sample of female students studied by Hamilton and Powers (1990) may explain why these students did not experience much occupational success in the first six months after graduation.

Selection bias has not been controlled in these studies. Students who work, who spend more time working, or who work at better jobs while in high school may also possess unobserved traits that lead to more favorable employment outcomes later. To correct for selection bias, it would be necessary to find other 'instrumental' variables that predict high school work experience but do not directly predict later employment outcomes. Such variables are hard to find. Ruhm (1993) tried using information about the student's geographic location during high school and subsequently, but these are likely to be highly correlated with each other, and the result was inconclusive. However, Ruhm did find that work experience during senior year had a positive effect on subsequent employment and earnings, while work experience during sophomore and junior years did not. This suggests that it is the senior-year work experience itself, rather than the student's predisposition to work, that accounts for the subsequent positive effects in the labor market.

Association Between Working Many Hours a Week and School Performance

Most studies, but not all, find that students who spend many hours a week in paid employment put in less time on homework, get lower grades or test scores, are more likely to drop out, or express less positive attitudes and aspirations about school. D'Amico (1984) found study time significantly lower, and likelihood of dropping out significantly higher, for white females and males who spent a larger proportion of weeks working twenty hours or more. Greenberger's and Steinberg's (1986) cross-sectional analysis of a small sample from Orange County, California found lower grades for students who worked more than fifteen hours in grade 10 or more than twenty hours in grade 11. Steinberg and Dornbusch (1991), in a larger sample from Wisconsin and northern California, found lowest self-reported grades for students who worked most hours. The same sample was analyzed by Steinberg, Fegley and Dornbusch (1993) controlling for 1987/88 work status (not working, working one-nineteen hours/week, working twenty or more hours/week) and also controlling for the 1987/88 lagged dependent variable in predicting self-reported grades and homework hours by work status group in 1988–89. They found homework hours and grades were lowest in the group working twenty hours or more. Yasuda (1990) also found lowest self-reported grades in the group working most hours. Barton (1989) found 1986 National Assessment of Educational Progress (NAEP) eleventh grade scores in math, science, history, literature and reading were lowest for students working most hours per week. Lillydahl's (1990) analysis of National Assessment of Economic Education sample found a negative coefficient on (hours/week) in predicting grades, implying lowest scores for those working most hours. Schill, McMartin and Meyer (1985) studied high school students in the state of Washington, finding lower self-reported grades for students working more than twenty hours than for those working one-twenty. Steel (1991) found hours/week employed in 1979 were negatively associated with weeks of enrollment in post-secondary education in 1980/81. Marsh (1991) analyzed the HSB 1980 sophomore cohort: those who worked during sophomore year were more likely to drop out before the spring of senior year, and among those still enrolled in 1982, hours worked in sophomore through senior years were negatively associated with the probability of going to college, standardized test scores, and attitudes/ aspirations toward school. Analysis of YIT data by Owens (1992) found seniors who worked more hours were less likely to go to college.

On the other hand, Greenberger and Steinberg's (1986) longitudinal analysis failed to confirm that working long hours leads to lower grades. Mortimer, Shanahan and Ryu's (1991) analysis of a sample from St. Paul found no significant relationship between grades and working more than fifteen hours/week. Hotchkiss (1986) found no significant relationship between hours of work and grades among a sample of students from Columbus, Ohio.

A study by Goldstein (1991) suggests that working students' grades may overstate their actual performance, because teachers lower their expectations for these students. Eighty-eight per cent of the teachers he interviewed felt that outside jobs had a negative impact on students' classroom performance. However, 60 per cent admitted they had changed the way they taught because of students' outside employment, 47 per cent said they had lowered their expectations, and 28 per cent admitted to lowering their standards for grading. Statistical analysis found no significant relationship between working and grades in this sample, from one high school.

Association Between Working a Moderate Number of Hours Per Week and School Performance

Most studies, but not all, find a *positive* association between working a moderate number of hours/week and school outcomes. D'Amico (1984) found the proportion of weeks spent working one to twenty hours/ week was associated with lower (i.e., better) class rank for white males, and with lower probability of dropping out for white males and females. Barton (1989) found the highest NAEP scores among students who worked less than six or eleven to fifteen hours per week. Lillydahl's regression contained a positive coefficient on the linear hours/week term, implying that students who work a moderate amount (thirteen-and-a-half hours, to be exact) get the best grades. Schill, McMartin, and Meyer (1985) found self-reported grades were higher for students who worked one to twenty hours than for those who were not working at all. Steel (1991) discovered that being employed in 1979 was positively associated with white students' enrollment in post-secondary education in 1980/81. Steinberg and Dornbusch (1991) found students working one to ten hours/week had slightly better grades than those who were not employed. Charner's and Fraser's (1987) review concluded that there seems to be a curvilinear relationship between hours/week and grades, with a 'magical cutoff' at twenty hours/week.

However, some studies have found a negative association between working a moderate number of hours per week and measures of school performance. Barton (1989) discovered NAEP scores were lowest among black eleventh graders who worked one to six hours/week, and among all students time spent on homework declines monotonically with employed hours/week. Greenberger and Steinberg (1986), in their longitudinal analysis, found that students reduced their homework time after they found jobs. Steinberg, Fegley and Dornbusch (1993) found a similar result: among students who were not employed in 1987/88, those who were employed one to nineteen hours per week in 1988/89 spent significantly less time on homework than those who were still not employed in the latter year, in an ANCOVA controlling for time spent on homework in the earlier year.

Although most studies of economic outcomes have not controlled for selection bias, some studies of educational outcomes have attempted to do so, in various ways. Steinberg, Fegley and Dornbusch (*ibid*) used students' prior work status as a stratifying variable, and controlled statistically for the lagged dependent variable, but still found significant negative associations between employed hours per week and school behavior. Hotchkiss (1986) controlled for lagged dependent variables and found no significant effect of working. Lillydahl (1990) used two-stage least-squares, the first stage of which included a tobit equation to predict work hours per week and a probit equation to predict whether the student planned to attend college; in the second stage she found significant linear and quadratic terms in work hours per week predicting grades. Mortimer, Shanahan and Ryu (1991) developed equations to predict grades and homework time, using a Heckman term 'estimated on the basis of background variables and the timing of first employment', in addition to the lagged dependent variables and other control variables: in these equations work hours per week ceases to be a significant predictor.

Comparison with Studies on Effects of Working While in College

A positive relation between working while in college and earnings a few years after college was observed in data from the NLS Young Men cohort (Stephenson 1981 and 1982; San, 1986). The relation between working and grades has variously been found to be: null (Ehrenberg and Sherman, 1987, analysis of NLS72; Bella and Huba, 1982, single institution); positive (Augenblick, Van De Water and Associates, 1987, survey in state of Washington; Hammes and Haller, 1983, single institution); and negative (Hay, Evans and Lindsay, 1970, single institution — but men in jobs related to field of study had significantly better grades than men in unrelated jobs). In contrast, there is a consistent negative relation between working and persistence in school, as estimated by Kohen, Nestel and Karmas (1978); Augenblick, Van De Water and Associates (1987); Ehrenberg and Sherman (1987 — but students working on campus are more likely to persist through graduation).

These results, as far as they go, are fairly consistent with findings on high school students. Unlike the high school studies, research at the college level has not focused on work hours per week.

New Findings from the NCRVE Longitudinal Study

New evidence on the effects of working while in high school comes from a longitudinal survey sponsored by the National Center for Research in Vocational Education (NCRVE). This survey is unique in having collected data on students' participation in co-op, school-based enterprise, and non-school-supervised work experience, as well as extensive information about qualitative characteristics of students' jobs. The sample discussed here came from one suburban and one urban school district in the midwest, and from one suburban and one rural district in the southeast. The districts were chosen because they all offered a fairly rigorous form of cooperative education. At each school, some students in the sample were participating in co-op, some in non-school-supervised jobs, some in school-based enterprises, and some were not working at all during senior year. Co-op students were deliberately oversampled to ensure a sufficient number for analysis. Data collection began in fall 1988 in two of the districts and in fall 1989 in the other two districts; the last wave of data collection took place in spring 1992. A complete description of the sample and survey procedures is given in Cagampang and others (1993).

Information from the fall and spring of senior year was used to classify students according to the nature of their current work experience. Some 40 per cent of the sample were enrolled in co-op during the fall or spring but did not report any other kind of work experience. Another 31 per cent were participating only in non-school-supervised employment (NSWE). One per cent were working only in school-based enterprise (SBE). Seven per cent participated in both co-op and SBE during the year; 3 per cent in NSWE and SBE; 2.5 per cent in co-op and NSWE; and 0.7 per cent did all three. Fourteen per cent reported no work of any kind in either fall or spring.

The fall and spring surveys asked students how many hours they worked during an average week. Students were asked to give the number of hours for weekdays and weekends separately, and the answers subsequently were added together. The mean for students who participated only in co-op was 24.5 hours, with a standard deviation (s.d.) of 8.7 hours. Students who enrolled in co-op and also participated in either NSWE or SBE worked an average of 26 hours (s.d. = 9.2). Those who did only NSWE reported an average of 21.9 hours (s.d. = 9.2). Evidently the co-op students worked longer hours. These differences are statistically significant, with $F(2, 557) = 8.19$, $p = 0.0003$. (Students who did not work are excluded from this analysis for obvious reasons; those who participated only in SBE are omitted because there were so

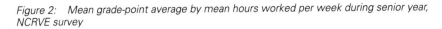

Figure 2: *Mean grade-point average by mean hours worked per week during senior year, NCRVE survey*

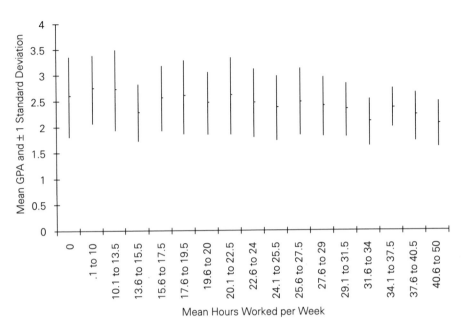

few of them; and those who combined SBE and NSWE are not included because they were too few to analyze separately and adding them to the NSWE category would violate the non-school-supervised criterion that defines this category.)

Grade-point averages (GPA) also differed among seniors with different kinds of work experience. GPA was computed from senior-year grades obtained from each student's official high school transcript. Top grades were in the NSWE-only group: mean = 2.66, s.d. = 0.68. Students who did not work at all had the next highest mean of 2.58 (s.d. = 0.77). Co-op students, and those who combined co-op with either NSWE or SBE, had the lowest means of 2.31 (s.d. = 0.57) and 2.27 (s.d. = 0.52), respectively. These differences are highly significant, with $F(3, 505)$ = 13.2, $p < 0.0001$.

The relationship between GPA and hours worked per week is shown in figure 2, the data for which are given in table 3. Students were divided into groups of roughly similar size according to the number of hours they worked during senior year. The mean GPA for each group is marked with a dash (—), and the vertical line next to each dash shows the standard deviation of GPA within the group. The result-

Table 3: Mean grade-point average and mean hours worked per week during senior year, NCRVE survey

Interval of hours per week	Mean GPA	Standard dev. of GPA	N of students in interval
0	2.61	0.79	39
1 to 10	2.76	0.66	33
10.1 to 13.5	2.73	0.77	33
13.6 to 15.5	2.30	0.54	25
15.6 to 17.5	2.57	0.62	36
17.6 to 19.5	2.57	0.72	30
19.6 to 20	2.45	0.63	51
20.1 to 22.5	2.61	0.73	33
22.6 to 24	2.46	0.68	33
24.1 to 25.5	2.36	0.62	31
25.6 to 27.5	2.48	0.66	29
27.6 to 29	2.39	0.57	30
29.1 to 31.5	2.31	0.52	26
31.6 to 34	2.05	0.48	24
34.1 to 37.5	2.34	0.39	25
37.6 to 40.5	2.16	0.46	15
40.6 to 50	2.01	0.45	18

ing picture shows GPA is highest among students who work a small number of hours each week, and lowest for those who work the most. This is consistent with previous research described in the preceding section.

More important than high school grades is what happens to students after they leave high school. At the time of the last survey in spring, 1992, 52 per cent of these seniors from the graduating classes of 1989 and 1990 were combining work with some kind of further schooling, 25 per cent were working but not in school, 18 per cent were in school but not working, and 6 per cent were neither working nor enrolled in school. The percentage in school was lower, and the percentage working was higher, than in nationally representative samples because the NCRVE survey deliberately over-sampled co-op students, who are more likely than other students to work and less likely to pursue post-secondary education.

Enrollment in post-secondary education as of 1992 was strongly related to high school grades, as one would expect. The former high school seniors who were combining work with further schooling had the highest GPA as seniors: mean = 2.66, s.d. = 0.61. GPAs were very nearly as high among those who went on to post-secondary education but were not working in 1992: mean = 2.63, s.d. = 0.68. GPAs were substantially lower among those who were working but not in school, or who were neither working nor in school: means = 2.19 and 2.12 (s.d.

Table 4: Percentage of NCRVE seniors from the classes of 1989 and 1990 participating in specified activities in spring 1992 by type of work experience during senior year

	Activity in Spring, 1992			
Senior work status	Work only	School only	Work and school	No work, no school
Co-op only (n = 195)	33	16	47	4
NSWE only (n = 171)	14	17	66	3
Co-op with NSWE or SBE (n = 52)	31	11	56	2
No work (n = 51)	18	33	22	27
Total (n = 469)	24	18	52	6

Table 5: Type of post-secondary school attended by NCRVE seniors from the classes of 1989 and 1990, by type of work experience during senior year

	Type of school attended in 1992		
Type of work experience during senior year	Vocational school	Two-year college	Four-year college
Co-op only (n = 118)	39	36	25
NSWE only (n = 137)	13	23	64
Co-op with NSWE or SBE (n = 33)	33	43	24
No work (n = 26)	11	31	58
Total (n = 314)	24	31	45

= 0.58 and 0.53), respectively. The difference is highly significant, with $F(3, 376) = 14.8$, $p < 0.0001$.

Employment in 1992 and participation in post-secondary education were also related to type of work experience during senior year, as shown in table 4. Former co-op students were more likely than other groups to be working but not in school. Former NSWE students were the most likely to be combining work with further schooling. Individuals who did not report working during senior year were more likely than others either to be in post-secondary school and not working, or neither working nor in school. These differences are highly significant: Pearson chi-square = 83.5 with 9 degrees of freedom, $p < 0.00001$. This corroborates the finding from previous research summarized above, that high school co-op students are relatively unlikely to enroll in post-secondary education.

Those co-op students who did attend post-secondary school were relatively likely to enroll in vocational schools or two-year colleges, and less likely to go to four-year colleges, as table 5 shows. The group most likely to attend four-year college were former seniors whose only work experience during senior year was NSWE. The differences are highly significant: Pearson chi-square = 52.7 with 6 degrees of freedom, $p < 0.00001$.

Evidently, students who held co-op jobs during their senior year seem to have been more work-oriented, and less oriented toward further schooling, than their classmates who worked only in non-school-supervised jobs or who did not work at all. This is consistent with previous findings from the NCRVE baseline data, which compared co-op and NSWE students' perceptions of their jobs during senior year. The co-op students more frequently indicated at the time that their jobs were interesting, gave them opportunities to learn, made use of what they had learned in school, and were related to their desired careers (Stone, Stern, Hopkins and McMillion, 1990).

Correspondingly, the follow-up data now reveal that former seniors who went to work but not to school in 1992 were more likely to have said that their senior-year jobs:

let them do the things they did best;
taught them new skills that would be useful in their future work;
influenced their career choice;
made them want to quit school as soon as possible;
gave them a chance to be helpful to others; and
were very challenging.

Chi-square tests showed the senior-year answers to each of these questions were significantly associated with whether individuals were in school, working, doing both, or doing neither in 1992.

These results are logically compatible with two different causal interpretations. Analysis of the NCRVE data, or of other data, have not yet provided a clear test of whether one or the other of these explanations accounts for more of the evidence. First, co-op students and others who find jobs that they like during senior year may have a greater probability, as a result, of going to work after high school and not continuing in post-secondary education. Alternatively, students who are already interested in going to work and not to post-secondary education may be more likely to enroll in co-op while they are in high school and also to make more positive statements about their high school jobs. Both explanations may contribute to the observed linkages between co-op participation, positive reports about senior-year jobs, and subsequent participation in work but not post-secondary education. However, these two interpretations have different implications for educational policy and practice. The first one implies that co-op and good jobs for students may divert them away from possibly beneficial participation in post-secondary education — may promote short-term well-being but reduce longer-term opportunities — and should therefore be limited or redesigned to avoid this harmful effect. The second interpretation assumes that students already know what is in their own best interest, and implies that co-op and good jobs should be promoted to help students achieve their own purposes.

Further evidence from the NCRVE survey about the monetary benefits from senior-year jobs a few years later can be found in the information on 1992 wages. Individuals who were working in 1992 were asked their hourly wage or, if paid by the week, their weekly earnings, which were then divided by hours worked per week in 1992. The sample mean was $6.19, s.d. = $1.98. Ordinary least-squares regression analysis was done with wage as the dependent variable. The predictors were:

- whether the individual had participated in co-op during senior year with a written training plan;
- entent to which (on a four-point scale) the senior-year job was said at the time to teach new skills that would be useful in the student's future work;
- cumulative grade-point average at the end of senior year;
- number of hours per week worked on the senior-year job; and
- whether the individual was male.

Regressions were estimated first for all 1989 and 1990 seniors, then for those who were not enrolled in post-secondary education in 1992. F statistics for both regressions were significant: $p = 0.0012$ for the first, $p = 0.0145$ for the second. As table 6 shows, the only statistically significant predictor of 1992 wages for the group as a whole was gender. However, grades and opportunity to learn useful skills on the job during senior year were also significant, in addition to gender, as predictors for the not-enrolled groups.

The differences between the two sets of regression coefficients in table 6 can be explained as follows. First, why is a high grade-point average associated with a higher wage within the not-enrolled group, but not in the whole group? The reason is that the not-enrolled have lower grades but higher wages compared to their former classmates who did enroll in post-secondary education. In the regression for the whole group, this negative correlation of grades and wages between the enrolled and not-enrolled attenuates the positive correlation between grades and wages within the not-enrolled group, leaving a nonsignificant regression coefficient of 0.080. There is a similar but smaller

Table 6: Regressions for hourly wage in 1992, NCRVE seniors from classes of 1989 and 1990: unstandardized coefficients (t-statistics in parentheses)

Predictor	Whole group	Not in post-secondary
Co-op	0.511	−0.123
	(1.92)	(−0.29)
Job thought to teach useful skills		
for future work	0.190	0.368*
	(1.57)	(2.02)
Grades	0.080	0.693*
	(0.41)	(2.10)
Hours worked per week senior year	0.017	0.037
	(1.17)	(1.63)
Male	0.770**	0.902*
	(3.07)	(2.25)
Constant	4.558**	3.131**
	(6.04)	(2.95)
R^2	0.092	0.197
n	213	69

* $p < 0.05$
** $p < 0.01$

attenuation in the whole group of the coefficient on the variable reflecting opportunities to learn useful skills on the job during senior year. In contrast, the coefficient on co-op participation is larger in the whole group than in the not-enrolled group. The reason is that the not-enrolled are more likely to have participated in co-op than their former classmates who attended post-secondary schools. Since the not-enrolled also have higher wages in 1992, this contributes to a positive (but not quite significant) correlation in the whole group between co-op participation and wages. However, within the not-enrolled group alone there is virtually no association between 1992 wages and participation in co-op two or three years earlier.

Apart from the effects of participation in a co-op program, table 6 also indicates that students obtain higher wages after graduation if they have held jobs where they thought they were learning useful skills. This is consistent with findings from NLSY data (Stern and Nakata, 1989). It could mean that students with more energy, ambition, or other traits not accounted for in this analysis are able both to find jobs that teach them more while they are in school and also to find better paying jobs later on, compared to students who lack these traits. But the findings in table 6 could also mean simply that skills obtained while working as a student pay off in higher wages later on. This second interpretation implies that, in designing or evaluating work experience for students, it is important to go beyond programmatic labels such as co-op or youth apprenticeship, and to consider qualitative characteristics of students' jobs, particularly the amount of opportunity to learn new skills.

Although the regression coefficient on co-op participation in the whole group does not quite meet customary standards of statistical significance (t = 1.96, p = 0.05) the bivariate association between co-op participation and 1992 wages does. The mean wage for former co-op participants was $6.40 (s.d. = $1.77) and $5.94 (s.d. = $2.19) for non-participants. This yields a t statistic of 2.04 with 308 degrees of freedom; p = 0.04.

However, on closer inspection the wage advantage for former co-op participants is statistically significant only for individuals whose 1992 employer was the same as their employer during senior year. Among this sub-sample who did not change employers, the mean wage in 1992 was $6.71 (s.d. = $1.32) for the former co-op students, and $6.09 (s.d. = $1.77) for the others. This gives a t statistic of 2.04 with 109 degrees of freedom; p = 0.04. In the sub-sample who did change employers, the mean wage in 1992 was $6.22 (s.d. = $1.96) among former co-op students, and $5.85 (s.d. = $2.40) among the non-co-op group. This gives a t statistic of 1.18 with 197 degrees of freedom, which is not statistically significant. This replicates the finding of Stern and Stevens (1992). As stated above, it seems that co-op leads to higher wages if individuals stay with the same employers, but not if they change. The benefits of co-op appear not to be portable.

In brief, these findings indicate that co-op participation yields a short-term advantage but also possibly a longer-term disadvantage. The short-term advantage is a gain in wages for co-op participants, compared to non-participants, as long as they stay with their co-op employer. The possible disadvantage is that co-op may steer students away from post-secondary education, and especially from four-year colleges, thus reducing their chances for later career mobility. These effects of co-op are not necessarily the result of the program structure itself. They probably reflect the fact that the co-op programs studied here, like most co-op programs in high schools, are tied to traditional vocational education programs that aim primarily to prepare students for immediate employment, not for further education.

Career Counseling and Job Placement

Career counseling and job placement services have sometimes been provided as part of vocational education in high schools. Section 322 of the Perkins Act specifically authorizes states and localities to 'improve,

Table 7: Guidance, counseling and job placement services provided by secondary schools to special populations enrolled in vocational education: Percentages*

	Proportion served 1991/92				Change in service since 1990/91		
	All	**Most**	**Some**	**None**	**More**	**Less**	**Same**
Disabled: guidance and counseling on transition to further education or employment	44.1	26.5	24.2	5.2	32.8	1.3	65.9
Disabled: job placement services	19.7	16.9	40.0	23.4	19.2	1.6	79.2
Educationally disadvantaged: guidance and counseling on transition to further education or employment	33.6	26.4	33.6	6.5	25.1	1.5	73.4
Educationally disadvantaged: job placement services	16.7	20.5	45.5	17.3	17.3	1.9	80.8
Economically disadvantaged: guidance and counseling on transition to further education or employment	30.2	25.3	36.1	8.4	23.6	0.7	75.6
Economically disadvantaged: job placement services	19.5	21.0	46.0	13.5	19.2	1.4	79.4
Limited English Proficient: guidance and counseling on transition to further education or employment	28.7	21.8	36.2	13.3	19.9	2.1	77.9
Limited English Proficient: job placement services	12.3	7.9	42.3	37.5	11.3	2.1	86.7

* Denominator includes only schools that report enrolling each special population in vocational education.

expand, and extend career guidance and counseling programs to meet the career development, vocational education, and employment needs of vocational education students and potential students'.

These services can target a broad range of students. In a survey of programs which emphasize these components, the following categories of students were identified by at least one program as its focus: Handicapped, disadvantaged, at-risk, limited English proficiency, teen parents, migrants, displaced homemakers, as well as the entire school population (California Institute on Human Services, 1990). The career counseling and job placement approaches, clearly, are thought to be quite versatile in the kinds of students they can benefit. The Perkins Act requires that career counseling and job placement services be offered to special populations of students enrolled in vocational education, and table 7 (from Stern, 1992a) indicates that the availability of such services is widespread. Coverage is not universal, but it is expanding.

Examples of the career counseling and job placement components of school-to-work programs are less distinctive than more general approaches to the school-to-work problem. Indeed, career counseling and job placement are examples of dimensions upon which programs are created. The job placement element of a program, for example, generally involves for participating students help with writing a resume, job search skills, and interview techniques. In addition, students are informed of job leads — or, in some cases, placed in a position by program staff. For example, the Boulder Valley Teen Parenting Program offers to teen mothers the opportunity to continue high school by providing pre- and post-natal health services, transportation, on-site child care — but also career assessment and job placement counseling (Parmerlee-Greiner, 1993).

An example of a more aggressive approach to job placement can be found at Duncan Polytechnical High School in Fresno, California. In this four-year vocational magnet school the administration has created a 'job developer' position, who is responsible for reviewing want-ads, calling on local businesses, attending job fairs, and informing students of job opportunities that exist. In addition, students at Duncan are counseled on job finding skills, such as telephone etiquette, resume writing and interviewing techniques (California Institute on Human Services, 1990).

Evaluating the contribution that career counseling and job placement make to school-to-work programs is difficult. Since these features rarely stand on their own, it is not always possible to isolate their effects from other features of the program (for example, workplace-based skill training, academic instruction, and mentoring). A set of '70,001' program sites, however, which emphasize the pre-employment services of career counseling and job placement have been evaluated (Lah *et al.*, 1983). Participating students were aged 16 to 21, over 80 per cent minority, 60 per cent women, and almost all high school dropouts. Participant and comparison groups (not randomly assigned) were evaluated. The findings were that 70,001 participants earned significantly higher wages than non-participants, and enjoyed a higher probability of finding employment. These differences, however, did not persist: The positive short-term effects seemed to decay in the case of female participants, and disappear for male participants. There was, in fact, no evidence of long-term positive effects (twenty-four to forty months after program intake). These findings indicate that such programs do seem to place youth in private sector jobs, allowing them to experience earnings gains; but that eventually comparison group members will get jobs on their own, and the advantages enjoyed by participants will disappear. The researchers concluded by speculating that career counseling and job placement programs, at least in the case of disadvantaged youth, are only limited steps in a series of necessary interventions.

Additional services subsequent to pre-employment training might be necessary to sustain economic gains.

Despite the difficulty of evaluating the effectiveness of career counseling and job placement programs *per se*, the literature on the school-to-work transition continues to identify these as important features of effective practice. In both research and policy documents, counseling and placement efforts have been treated as necessary, if not sufficient, elements of school-to-work programs (for example, Weber, 1987; Bishop, 1988; William T. Grant Foundation, 1988).

Mentoring Programs

The concept of mentoring is becoming increasingly popular in both the school and the workplace as a means to improve educational and work outcomes. At the moment there exists a noticeable mentoring movement, in which 'mentoring' is well on the way to becoming a buzzword — and losing a specific definition which makes it possible to describe and evaluate this approach to education (Freedman and Jaffe, 1992).

Mentoring has been defined, most generally, as a relationship between a young person and an adult in which the adult offers support and guidance as the youth goes through a difficult period, enters a new area of experience, takes on important tasks, or attempts to correct an earlier problem. Mentoring is thought to be useful in particular for providing positive adult contacts for youth who are isolated from adults in their schools, homes, communities, and workplaces (Flaxman, Ascher and Harrington, 1988).

The new importance of mentoring in youth programs is partly a function of the conditions in which young people increasingly live in America — in urban America in particular. The widespread family breakdown, erosion of neighborhood ties, and time demands of parent work have created a situation in which few young people have even one significant close relationship with a non-parental adult before actually reaching adulthood (Steinberg, 1991). For inner-city youth the problem of having positive adult role models is compounded by the relatively higher rates of single-parent homes, the existence of fewer working adults, the strength of youth gangs, and more prevalent substance abuse (Wilson, 1987). Mentorship programs for youth have been designed to help fill this need for positive adult role models, support and guidance. The issue to be addressed in the following review of research, therefore, is the extent to which mentorship has been able to fill these needs.

Mentoring programs aimed at facilitating the school-to-work transition and related issues, such as dropout prevention and the transition from school to college, have been implemented by four kinds of organizations (Crockett and Smink, 1991): schools, community organizations, business-education partnerships, and higher-education institutions. The following are examples of some of these programs.

The school-based Norwalk Mentor Program began in 1986, and concentrates its efforts on potential high school dropouts (Weinberger, 1992). The signs used to indicate a high probability of dropping out of school, and therefore as criteria for admission to the program, include single-parent family status, poor school attendance, poor attitude in class, and a family history of substance abuse. The program consists of a number of steps, all of which are undertaken by program staff. (1) Mentors are recruited from the community and screened, (2) and then undergo an orientation and training program. As part of this phase selected mentors sign an agreement regarding their responsibilities in the program. (3) Mentors are matched with participating students. (4) Mentors and students meet in weekly sessions on campus. Initially program staff emphasize informing mentors about activities which are likely to cultivate effective relationships (i.e. 'ice-breakers'). (5) The program is evaluated through surveys of mentors and students. And (6), all participants mark the year's end with 'celebrations and renewal' activities. Program staff, however, do all that they can to ensure that mentor-student relationships do not end at the close of the school year, but instead continue in the summer months and into the following year.

Community-based mentoring programs have been in existence for some time in this country. The Big Brothers/Big Sisters programs, for example, which involve mentor-like relationships, have been in existence for ninety years. An example of a program which aims more specifically to smooth the transition from school to work is the Greenville Urban League's Partnership Program Mentorship Component. This program offers minority students in grades ten through twelve the mentorship of a black professional in the Greenville community. Students are encouraged to meet with mentors in the workplace, to both observe the world of work and to discuss issues. Another example is the Oregon Community Mentorship Program, a state-wide effort resulting from Oregon's recent Student Retention Initiative. The goal of the program is to keep students in school, and also to provide orientation to the world of work. The first step in getting the program operating is to establish local committees of education and business groups, who then proceed to outline a program, select students, recruit mentors, and coordinate the program. Thus, although the mentoring is essentially a state-wide effort, each mentor program is geared to the needs of participating communities.

Project Step-Up is an example of a mentoring program initiated through a business-education partnership. The program was begun in 1985 at Aetna Life and Casualty to assist disadvantaged teens in the greater Hartford area make the transition successfully from school to work. Participating students start the program at age 15, having been referred to the program by school personnel. Aetna interviews the students, and accepts a percentage of this group. Students begin the program by attending fifteen two-hour classes after school over a five-month period on the Aetna site. Classes cover a range of subjects, including business ethics, business writing, basic math and computer literacy. Students who complete these courses are guaranteed jobs with Aetna. Once on the job, students are assigned Aetna employees as mentors, who are expected to offer personal counseling, help with homework, and a role model. Upon graduating from high school, most participating students join Aetna and make the transition to permanent, full-time employment. Other students enroll in a post-secondary institution, and are guaranteed summer employment by Aetna.

College and university-based efforts to assist disadvantaged youth have become more common recently. A 1989 study found over 1700 mentoring or tutoring programs sponsored by higher education institutions for primary and secondary students across the country (Reisner, 1989). Mentoring is the focus of 17 per cent of these programs; and of these mentoring programs 27 per cent concentrate on secondary school students (Cahalan and Farris, 1990). There are, therefore, roughly 80 higher education-based mentoring programs for high school students across the country.

Career Beginnings is an example of this kind of mentoring program. Organized by the Center for Human Resources at Brandeis University, Career Beginnings is a national program for high school juniors from low-income families who have average attendance and academic records. The program is designed to serve, therefore, students who have the potential to succeed in school and the workforce, but are not doing so. The program operates in twenty-five projects in twenty-two cities nationally. In all Career Beginnings-sponsored programs at least half of the participating students must be economically disadvantaged, 80 per cent must be of the first generation in their families to attend college, and 45 per cent must be male. The program itself offers to students the mentorship of an adult; but also a quality summer job experience, job skills and college application training, and continuing guidance through their senior year and transition from school to college or work.

The programs described in the preceding paragraphs are all explicitly mentoring programs. It is important to note, however, that many mentoring programs exist as components of larger school-to-work efforts. Mentorships are a component of the career academy model in California (Stern, Raby and Dayton, 1992). Co-op programs, such as Oregon's Partnership Project in the retail and manufacturing industries, and the National Alliance of Business and Bank of America's Quality Connection banking program, also use mentorship as a key program ingredient. In addition, youth apprenticeship programs, such as the Youth Apprenticeship Demonstration Project in Broome County, New York, and Boston's Project ProTech, generally reflect the view that mentorship is an important feature of an effective school-to-work program.

Although the four types of mentoring programs illustrated above have important differences, stemming primarily from the perspective of the organization which operates the program, each type has in common the fundamental relationship of mentoring and a concern about the transition from school to work. Through mentoring students are exposed to career education (or at least to post-secondary options), which is thought to help students understand the expectations of employers about the attitudes, preparedness and skills required for work; as well as to give students the chance to see the application of school activities to subsequent life. In addition, many mentoring programs offer to youth assistance in obtaining summer and postgraduate jobs (US Department of Education, 1990). At the most basic level, mentoring programs offer to youth the support of an adult, without which the educational and vocational futures of an increasing percentage of youth are in doubt.

The popularity of mentorship in youth-serving programs belies the newness of the use of mentorship in a systematic way in these programs. Not surprisingly, therefore, there is little research evidence to support the intuition and anecdotal evidence of the success of mentoring for youth (Greim, 1992). The evidence that exists is mixed. The Adopt-A-Student program, for example, has been evaluated by several analysts. Stanwyck and Anson (1989) find that students who were assigned mentors were more likely than the comparison group to enroll in a post-secondary institution. Freedman (1991), however, asserts that participants are no more likely to graduate from high school or to be employed subsequently than students without mentors. Similarly, in the case of Career Beginnings, Moloney and Mckaughan (1990) argue that the majority of adults and youths in the program felt good about the mentoring experience, and could identify important benefits. Cave and Quint (1990), however, find that participating youth went on to college at only slightly higher rates than the control group.

Additional research indicates that youth and mentors form successful relationships in fewer than half of the matches made in the Campus Partners in Learning mentoring program (Tierney and Branch, 1992). Yet an evaluation of the Norwalk Mentor Program indicates that almost all mentors (96 per cent) report excellent or good relationships with their students, and 85 per cent feel that the relationship has made a positive impact on the student's life. This evaluation contained less subjective evidence, as well: 87 per cent of participating students show improved attendance, and 96 per cent show greater cooperation in class (Weinberger, 1992).

Despite the current lack of conclusive knowledge of whether and how mentor programs work, several analysts have begun to produce 'best practice' recommendations for future efforts (see Hamilton and Hamilton, 1990; Freedman, 1991; Greim, 1992; Styles and Morrow, 1992). Hamilton and Hamilton (1990), for example, have concluded that:

- Mentors should be recruited through organizations, and not on a one-at-a-time basis.
- Mentoring programs should concentrate on youth who need this kind of support and guidance.
- Mentors need clear goals in order to be effective.
- Mentors need continuing support from program staff.
- Mentoring needs a context, such as the workplace or the school site, in order to be meaningful to youth.

In summary, mentorship programs designed to assist in the school-to-work transition are becoming more popular. These programs enjoy several advantages over other approaches to this issue, including their relatively low cost, the directness of their intervention in the lives of youth, their simplicity, and their flexibility (Freedman, 1991). In addition, on a theoretical level, the need for mentorship programs, particularly for urban youth, has never been higher.

However, on an empirical level, the evidence is mixed. There has not been, as yet, a study which conclusively demonstrates the contribution that mentoring programs are thought to be capable of making. It is worth keeping in mind that mentoring programs create relationships that are but one of many influences on the youth involved (Freedman, 1991). Mentoring, in this sense, is a 'modest intervention'. Its power to substitute for missing adult figures is limited. Until more extensive research has been conducted, it is important that mentoring programs not be oversold; for that could lead to the diversion of attention from the causes of the problems these programs have been devised to ameliorate in the first place (Flaxman, Ascher and Harrington, 1988).

Note

1   We wish to thank the following individuals for their useful insights on youth apprenticeship: Mr. LaMarr Billups, Wisconsin Department of Industry, Labor and Human Relations; Professor Stephen Hamilton, Cornell University; Ms. Barbara Henrie, Minnesota Technology Inc.; Mr. Peter Jay, University of Minnesota; Ms. Alicia Philipps, Minnesota Department of Labor and Industry; Mr. Ronald Schertzer, Arkansas Vocational and Technical Division; and Ms. Sharon Wherley, Pennsylvania Youth Apprenticeship Program.

3 School-and-Work Programs in Two-Year Colleges

Two-year colleges are taking increasingly diverse roles in the delivery of job-related instruction. While it has always been the case that community, junior and technical colleges offered some vocational curricula, the range of direct linkages with outside organizations has become remarkably wide: At present, two-year colleges are engaged in cooperative education, work-study, tech-prep, community-based education, economic development services, JTPA training, faculty internships in industry, apprenticeship and pre-apprenticeship training, and contracted customized training for employers (Suchorski, 1987).

Cooperative education and apprenticeship are considered in this chapter; tech-prep in the next one. Table 8 shows the percentages of two-year institutions offering co-op and apprenticeship programs, and the percentages of students participating in them, as reported to the National Assessment of Vocational Education survey in 1992 (Stern, 1992a). Two-year institutions are classified as comprehensive community colleges, vocational-technical institutes, area vocational schools serving post-secondary students, or other. More than two out of three institutions offer cooperative education or work experience; there is no nationally consistent distinction between the two at the post-secondary level. Almost one institution in six offers the classroom component of apprenticeship training. Nearly nine out of ten two-year institutions also operate school-based enterprises, but the numbers of students involved are tiny. Even co-op/work experience and apprenticeship do not enroll very large numbers, accounting for only 2.25 and 1.39 per cent of enrollment, respectively.

Cooperative Education

Although evaluation of post-secondary co-op programs has been supported by the Higher Education Act (for example, see Fletcher, 1989),

Table 8: Prevalence of school-to-work programs in two-year public post-secondary institutions

	Comp. CC	Vo-tech	AVS	Other	Total
Number of institutions	675	175	72	68	993
Percentage* of institutions reporting presence of each program					
Co-op/work experience	75.85	54.86	52.78	39.71	67.88
Apprenticeship programs	16.89	18.29	9.72	4.41	15.71
School-based enterprises	88.89	90.29	84.72	89.71	88.82
Participating students as a percentage* of total enrollment					
Co-op/work experience	2.23	2.35	4.15	1.54	2.25
Apprenticeship programs	0.93	3.58	11.63	2.26	1.39
School-based enterprises	0.05	0.13	0.54	0.10	0.06
Participating students as a percentage* of full-time day enrollment					
Co-op/work experience	7.34	9.76	10.50	3.36	7.43
Apprenticeship programs	3.07	14.89	29.44	4.93	4.57
School-based enterprises	0.15	0.53	1.36	0.22	0.21

* Denominator includes institutions that did not respond to the question.

most of these evaluations have been done in four-year colleges. Evaluations of co-op in two-year colleges have been too sparse and too limited to permit any firm conclusions or generalizations. We summarize here the few studies we have found.

Siedenberg (1989b) has proposed a simple statistical model to isolate the impact of co-op education on students' initial wage after graduation. According to this model, the initial wage rate (W) that a graduate will receive is a function of her stock of human capital (H), a vector of personal characteristics and proxies for cognitive and affective traits (P), and labor market conditions (L). Formally,

$$W = f (H, P, L).$$

Using data from 840 co-op and non co-op students, Siedenberg found that co-op students received lower wages while in college, but after graduation their wages were no lower, or higher, than non co-op graduates. He concluded that 'participants in the co-op program had increased the quantity and quality of their human capital while at the college' (p. 26).

Heinemann (1988), an advocate of co-op education, described the benefits of a co-op program at LaGuardia College in New York. LaGuardia is the only two-year college in the US where co-op education is mandatory for all full-time students. The program consists of three, three-month, full-time co-op education assignments. Heinemann's data show that most students who complete their first co-op assignment go on to complete their degree. Employer evaluations reflect satisfied employers and enthusiastic and eager students. Approximately two-thirds of LaGuardia students continue their education (1983 data). The College is known for its co-op program and it is believed that it is because of co-op that enrollments have grown.

The research problem addressed by Krebs (1988) was the perceived usefulness of the co-op experience for graduates who entered the labor force. He included graduates from two different co-op programs in his survey, the Production and Operating Management (POM) program and Marketing Management (MAM) program. It is important to note that the sample was relatively small (N = 89), and that response rates were much lower for the MAM program (35 per cent versus 72 per cent for POM). The co-op in this study consisted of a two-day per week compulsory placement in a company. The independent variables measured in the study were: match between co-op experience and first job, challenge of work experience, and demands made by the instructor. The dependent variable, usefulness of co-op experience, measured how often after graduation the graduates reportedly used the skills and knowledge acquired in the co-op experience. Regression analysis showed that POM graduates considered their co-op experience more useful than did MAM graduates, controlling for other predictors. The match and challenge dimensions of the co-op experience were strongly correlated with reported usefulness. Demands made by the instructor were found to have little effect on the perceived usefulness. Women from the POM program were found to have considerably higher means on all variables than men, in either program.

Stern, Stone, Hopkins, McMillion and Cagampang (1992) used 1989 baseline post-secondary data from the NCRVE longitudinal survey to compare 228 co-op students in two-year colleges to 375 non-co-op students at the same colleges, who were employed in the same occupational categories. (Survey procedures are described in Cagampang and others, 1993.) The survey included questions about qualitative characteristics of the current job. Table 9 summarizes salient findings, which indicate that co-op students see a stronger connection between their present job and their expected career (statements 1a and 1b); express more interest in their current jobs (statements 2a and 2b); report more opportunity for learning in their current jobs (statements 3a and 3b); and see closer connection between school and work (statements 4a, 4b and 4c). Whether these qualitative differences in students' work experience contribute to subsequent educational or economic outcomes is not yet known.

Table 9: Differences between job perceptions of co-op and non-co-op students in two-year colleges

Statement	Co-op	Non-co-op
1a) Why did you want this job?		
Per cent 'It was a career move'	31.6	22.7
1b) Do you think that the things you are learning in your job will be useful to you in your later life?		
Per cent 'extremely' or 'very useful'	62.9	40.7
2a) How often do you feel that your job is meaningful and important?		
Per cent 'Often' or 'Almost always'	70.0	51.2
2b) Overall, how challenging do you consider your present job?		
Per cent 'Very' or 'Somewhat'	73.8	55.6
3a) Why did you want this job?		
Per cent 'To learn new skills'	58.8	44.5
3b) To what extent does your job teach you new skills that will be useful in your future work?		
Per cent 'Some' or 'A great deal'	74.6	54.9
4a) My job gives me a chance to practice what I learned in school.		
Per cent 'Somewhat' or 'Very true'	68.7	45.1
4b) What I have learned in my classes helps me do better on my job.		
Per cent 'Agree' or 'Strongly agree'.	68.9	48.0
4c) My job provides information about things I am studying in college.		
Per cent 'Agree' or 'Strongly agree'	64.3	29.2

Source: Stern, Stone, Hopkins, McMillion and Cagampang, 1992.

Apprenticeship

Two-year colleges are expected to play a major role in new youth apprenticeships (see Chapter 2) or tech-prep programs (see Chapter 4), based on the 2 plus 2 or 4 plus 2 model. In addition, two-year colleges have long been active in traditional apprenticeship programs.

The essential components of traditional apprenticeship have been summarized as follows: A supervised, structured training program which (a) combines on-the-job with related theoretical instruction for skilled employment; and is (b) sponsored by employers or labor/management groups; (c) the result of a legal contract leading to a Certificate of

Completion and official journeyperson status; (d) a tangible and sizable investment on the part of the program sponsor; (e) a wage-paying activity, at least during the on-the-job phase of the program, in accordance with a predefined wage progression scale; (f) a training strategy in which participants learn by working under the direct supervision of masters of the craft or trade; and (g) a written agreement in which the apprentice can expect to be hired by the sponsor upon completion of the program, and the sponsor is obligated to hire the apprentice (William T. Grant Foundation, Commission on Work, Family, and Citizenship, 1992).

Over the past decade two-year colleges have managed to fit into this complicated set of requirements by offering, in a way satisfactory to all parties involved, the theoretical components of apprenticeship training. That is, while the sponsor provides the job-specific training at the work site, the college provides the general training related to the craft or trade. The apprentice-sponsoring organizations which enter such agreements with two-year colleges presuppose that some amount of literacy, numeracy, and fluency, as well as some familiarity with the natural and physical sciences, are prerequisites for expertise in any particular field (Casner-Lotto, 1988).

Two-year college involvement in any particular apprenticeship program is typically a result of a three-way partnership between a corporation, the relevant trade union, and the college itself. Union involvement is not a necessity in arranging an apprentice-like training program; such 'non-joint' (apprenticeship programs, however, with the exception of the auto industry's mechanic training programs, have not been successful over the long term. The tie between employers and the college have generally failed to remain close enough to sustain the training program (Conklin, 1987). Occasionally a professional organization, such as the Oregon Precision Metal Fabricators Association, and the National Tooling and Machining Association, will take a leading role in the partnership (Liston and Ward, 1984; Skinner, 1990). Of course, both the state and federal apprenticeship agencies and the state Department of Education must approve the apprenticeship program and the course work provided, respectively.

The majority of partnerships between two-year colleges and industry in apprenticeship training exist in established trades such as shipfitting, machining, pipefitting, and sheet metal working. Litton Industrial Products in Massachusetts, for example, has formed a partnership with area community colleges to help train its apprentices in the metal cutting tool industry (Tuholski, 1982). The maritime industry, in particular, relies upon its long-standing apprenticeship programs in the face of the current labor market situation: The industry is beset by severe literacy problems among shipyard workers, while, at the same time, technical requirements for the work are increasing. The equivalent of two post-secondary years of education and training are now required for the majority of shipyard work (Cantor, 1992). The US Navy has integrated two-year college course work into its formal four-year apprenticeship programs at each of its eight domestic shipyards (Cantor, 1988). These programs are generally quite large, as all but one of the Navy sites trains over 150 apprentices at any given time. Several of the programs consist of over 500 trainees. Tidewater Community College in Norfolk, Virginia, and Trident Technical College in Charleston, South Carolina, are among the leaders in these federal shipyard partnerships (Cantor, 1992).

Private sector shipyard apprenticeship training has also moved toward the community college partnership model. Norfolk Shipbuilding and Drydock, NASSCO, Ingalls, Bath Iron Works, and the Avondale Shipyard have each initiated programs of this kind. Thomas Nelson Community College provides on-site trade theory classes, advanced technical training, and general education courses as part of the Newport News Shipbuilding and Drydock Company's prestigious four-year apprenticeship program (*ibid.*), and the Community College of Rhode Island offered classroom training as part of the apprenticeship program of the Electric Boat Division of the General Dynamics Corporation (Liston and Ward, 1984).

More recent community college-employer partnerships have developed in other areas. The construction and fire fighting sectors, for example, are cultivating community college involvement in their apprenticeship and pre-apprenticeship training. The International Union of Operating Engineers (IUOE) and the International Brotherhood of Electrical Workers (IBEW) Local #3 in Flushing, NY, two construction industry unions, are working with contractors and area community colleges to offer three- and four-year apprenticeship programs leading to associate degrees. The IBEW Local #3 collaborates with Empire State College, and the IUOE collaborates with community colleges nationwide. In California, sixty-two community colleges offer fire service programs. Many are part of dual-enrollment apprenticeship programs, generally as part of the academy process (Cantor, 1992).

It is the automotive industry, however, that has been at the forefront of using two-year colleges for the educational needs of industry (Conklin, 1987). In order to meet the steady demand for auto repair mechanics, most of the major American and Japanese manufacturers have forged links with their local auto dealers, the dealers' trade associations, a few independent repair garages, and community colleges. It is estimated that General Motors, and subsequently Ford, Chrysler, Nissan, Toyota and Honda now operate over 500 apprenticeship programs involving two-year colleges throughout the United States and Canada (Cantor, 1991).

Although there is some variety in the industries that have created links with two-year colleges in apprenticeship training, colleges tend to take a similar role in these partnerships. The training normally takes place in college facilities, and is offered by college faculty. If a training class is sufficiently large or specialized, however, it might take place in company facilities. The Dean or Director of Vocational Education at the college receives a rough outline of the course from the employer (or from an employer/union training advisory board), and then prepares a curriculum for review and feedback (Casner-Lotto, 1988).

The apprentices in the program generally work on alternating schedules, i.e. working full-time for a period of months, and then studying full-time. The apprenticeship might consist of several such cycles. In GM's Automotive Services Excellence Program (ASEP), apprentices participate in a six-part cycle consisting of five to eight weeks of full-time school, and then five to eight weeks on the job. Apprentices work an eight-hour day on both cycles, beginning at 7:30 a.m. (*ibid.*). There are also examples of 'parallel' training programs, where apprentices put in classroom time after work. In a Pennsylvania machine technology program, for example, trainees spend two nights each week at a community college over the course of their three-year apprenticeship (Whitworth, 1982).

The classroom component of the apprenticeship training usually consists of both general and technical courses. In fact, most apprenticeship programs linked to two-year colleges are constructed to allow trainees to earn both a certificate of completion for the apprenticeship program as well as an associate degree from the college. The Navy shipyard program, for example, consists of the following courses: Expository writing, technical writing, arithmetic, chemistry, physics, a social science elective, drafting and blueprint reading (Cantor, 1988). The GM mechanic training program consists of state-of-the-art automotive theory courses, as well as courses in English, mathematics, history and psychology (Casner-Lotto, 1988). Rancho Santiago Community College's offerings on behalf of the Santa Ana Fire Department consist of eight core courses which are prerequisites for fire fighter certification. These classes also provide twenty-four units toward an associate degree in Fire Science Technology (Cantor, 1992). There are some apprenticeship programs that do not require the general education courses that are required as part of community college degree programs. Nearly all, however, offer incentives of some kind to encourage apprentices to take advantage of the college partnership by completing a degree program, in addition to the apprenticeship.

The college component of apprenticeship programs is shared among the parties involved. Trainees normally pay the standard college tuition for the courses they take, as well as paying for their books and tools (the latter costing upwards of $1000, in many cases). The sponsoring organization supplies equipment, manuals, uniforms and, of course, the wages for the on-the-job phase of training. The college provides instructors, the classroom and shop space, and administrative expenses (Casner-Lotto, 1988). Many training programs are more extensively supported by the sponsoring corporation or trade association, however. As part of the Community College of Rhode Island and General Dynamics' partnership, the company paid the full tuition of trainees, as well as a stipend for books and supplies (Liston, 1986). Funding for the IUOE and IBEW apprenticeship programs is supplemented by a journeyman's wage tax levied by employers. In the case of the IBEW program, the New York State Department of Labor also enters the funding picture, by providing $1.00 per training hour per apprentice. The Newport News Shipbuilding and Drydock Company pays all training costs for its apprentices, including college fees (Cantor, 1992). And, in perhaps the most generous of these kinds of programs, Chrysler Motor Corporation provides to its mechanics-in-training a $1500 grant toward educational costs, a salary of 160 per cent of the sponsoring dealership's minimum wage during both phases of training, and a $.50 per hour raise after each semester. In addition, Chrysler places $1.00 for every hour worked and studied by the trainee in escrow — the entire amount to be awarded to the trainee upon completion of the program, at which time he or she is guaranteed two years of full-time employment (Cantor, 1991).

The selection process for these apprenticeship partnerships is often quite rigorous: applications can far outnumber available places (Tuholski, 1982). The IBEW Local #3 apprenticeship program, for example, receives 2000–4000 applications annually for its roughly 700 apprenticeship positions (Cantor, 1992). Recruitment is normally undertaken by the future employer as well as the college, often through area secondary schools. Apprentices attracted in this way are uncommon among all American apprentices, however, where the average age is twenty-seven years (Stern, 1990).

Employers are seeking literate, motivated and mechanically able individuals. Sponsoring organizations use interviews and ability tests in the selection process (Casner-Lotto, 1988; Cantor, 1992). Intellectual measures used in the selection of trainees include high school and college transcripts, and aptitude tests (Cantor, 1992). The apprenticeship selection process has not always been equitable in its treatment of some populations, particularly women. In response, a pre-apprenticeship program has begun in Oregon, with the expressed goal of increasing the percentage of women in apprenticeship programs (which stood at 3.4 per cent as of 1987). Students in the program, located at Portland Community College, go through a curriculum of machinery, electronics, construction, carpentry, and even weight training in preparation for traditional apprenticeship (Portland Community College, 1991).

The costs and benefits of these two-year college and industry partnerships in apprenticeship training are relatively straightforward. The costs to the trainee can be significant, including tuition (usually $400–$500 per semester), and tools, room and board, if necessary, in addition to the opportunity cost of their time. Occasionally the employer covers out-of-pocket costs. The benefits to trainees include certification leading to journeyperson status from the sponsoring agency and the state, an associate degree in some field of applied science, and a strong likelihood of employment (Casner-Lotto, 1988; Conklin, 1987; Whitworth, 1982). Lynch (1992) estimated from NLSY data that the apprentices' rate of return on their investment averaged 13 per cent, which is higher than the average rate of return to a year in college.

Costs to the employer stem from wages paid to the trainee, as well as the equipment supplied to the college for training purposes. Benefits that are commonly expected from apprenticeship training partnerships include an increased supply of workers with improved communications skills and up-to-date technical skills, occasional retraining of displaced workers, and employee loyalty, all at a lower cost to the employer than if the training program were undertaken entirely under company auspices (Cantor, 1991; Casner-Lotto, 1988; Skinner, 1990). Colleges benefit from such partnerships with industry insofar as they are able to provide vocational and technical courses at a cost which is less than the fees and public subsidies they receive. Whether these subsidies are productive investments for taxpayers depends on the amount of taxable economic activity that is attributable to the existence of the apprenticeship program.

Despite the efforts of community, junior and technical colleges to continue to meet industry's needs by providing inexpensive, flexible, and often high-quality additions to training programs (Casner-Lotto, 1988), the future of such relationships is unknown. In California, for example, as of 1984, community colleges accounted for 75 per cent of the apprenticeship instruction done by educational institutions. By 1987, however, two-year colleges reportedly accounted for only 51 per cent of such instruction (Farland and Anderson, 1988). Apparently in California the sponsors of apprenticeship programs in the 1980s were turning more to regional vocational programs and adult schools to provide the classroom component.

Career Counseling and Job Placement

Career counseling and job placement offices of some kind have become nearly universal on two-year community and technical college campuses. For students from special populations enrolled in federally supported vocational education, the Perkins Act requires that schools provide individual career counseling and job placement assistance. The National Assessment of Vocational Education (NAVE) survey found that the great majority of two-year public post-secondary institutions do in fact report that they provide these services, as shown in table 10 (from Stern, 1992a).

While, traditionally, two-year colleges have done a more complete job of providing job placement than career counseling services (Hafer, 1982), table 10 indicates that counseling services have recently become more of a priority for these colleges.

Two related conclusions have been reached about guidance and placement programs which suggest that current practice can be improved. First, the same NAVE survey found that the major responsibility for finding jobs for vocational/technical graduates in general (not only special populations) falls on students themselves, with help from their particular instructors, and less help from job placement services. Table 11 illustrates this finding.

Second, counseling and placement programs have been more successful at helping those students who want to move on to further education than students who want to move into the labor market. A survey of Michigan community colleges revealed that for most guidance programs, perceived strengths are educational counseling and program planning/course selection. Weaknesses tend to be in job placement and career vocational counseling (Manley *et al.*, 1986). The preceding two findings suggest that those who have already experienced success in the academic context — the academically able and those intending to transfer to four-year colleges — are better served by two-year college counseling and placement programs than those who have been less successful in the school and college environment. This

Table 10: Guidance, counseling, and job placement services provided by two-year public post-secondary institutions to special populations enrolled in occupational/technical programs: Percentages*

	Service provided in 1990/91	Trend in service since 1990/91:		
		More	Less	Same
Disabled: guidance and counseling on transition to further education or employment	92.0	39.2	1.9	58.9
Disabled: job placement services	82.1	27.1	2.3	70.6
Disadvantaged†: guidance and counseling on transition to further education or employment	91.6	39.5	2.5	58.0
Disadvantaged†: employability and/or job search	86.3	35.0	2.4	62.6
Disadvantaged†: paid employment through a school-coordinated program (for example, co-op)	48.7	12.7	2.4	84.9
Disadvantaged†: a stipend or subsidized employment in conjunction with occupational/technical education	17.0	5.9	1.0	93.1
Limited English proficient: guidance and counseling on transition to further education or employment	84.4	29.1	1.7	69.2
Limited English proficient: job placement services	75.5	21.7	2.3	76.0
Single parents, single pregnant women, or displaced homemakers: child care	66.3	24.7	5.0	70.3
Single parents, single pregnant women, or displaced homemakers: job placement services	83.8	29.9	2.7	67.4
Job placement in nontraditional fields to eliminate sex bias	57.0	25.3	2.0	72.6

* Denominator includes only schools that report enrolling each special population in vocational education.
† Includes educationally and economically disadvantaged.

Table 11: Role of agencies or individuals in finding training-related jobs for occupational/ technical program graduates from two-year public post-secondary institutions: Percentages*

	Large role	Moderate role	Slight role	No role
Institution's job placement service	38.5	32.9	16.7	12.0
Public employment service	9.9	35.3	42.3	12.5
Employer and trade organizations	10.8	32.4	39.2	17.6
Occupational/technical faculty in the specialty area	57.0	32.5	8.7	1.9
Other faculty	6.7	30.0	46.4	16.9
Guidance staff	10.5	32.5	39.5	17.5
Director of occupational/technical education	12.3	24.6	36.1	27.1
Student him- or herself	80.1	16.6	3.2	0.2

* Only institutions that responded to the question are included.

Figure 3: Features of a two-year college career guidance system

Basic features	Recommended features
Assessment aids	Career information workshops
Career resource materials	On-campus interviews
Counseling	Career day(s)
Follow-up study	Career-related courses for credit
Job listings	Credential file service for job applications
Job search workshops	
Transfer assistance	
Cooperative work experiences	

conclusion indicates that for many two-year colleges increased attention to counseling and placement practice is appropriate.

Several guides to 'best practice' in two-year college guidance counseling and job placement programs exist (for example, Hafer, 1982; Virginia State Council of Higher Education, 1987; Muha *et al.*, 1988). A report from Virginia, based on a survey of higher education in that state, offers a useful framework, summarized in Figure 3.

4   Relevance of Vocational Education to Subsequent Employment

Cooperative education, apprenticeship, or other school-and-work programs engage students in school and work during the same period of time. The relationship between school and work is concurrent. In addition, high schools and two-year colleges, particularly their vocational education programs, include preparation for work as a major part of their mission. If these school-for-work programs succeed, there should be a sequential connection between school and work. Evidence about this sequential link is reviewed in this chapter.

High Schools and Secondary Vocational Centers

Average Effects

The 1990 Perkins Act continues the traditional definition of vocational education as preparation for 'occupations requiring other than a baccalaureate or advanced degree' (section 521(41)). Since jobs that do require bachelor's or advanced degrees on average pay more than those that do not, this definition inevitably means that vocational education prepares people for relatively low-paying occupations. The 1991 Current Population Survey on sources of work-related training found that 'about 44 per cent of the workers who studied in high school vocational programs to qualify for their jobs were in administrative support occupations' — mainly secretaries, receptionists, bookkeepers, typists and clerks — 'and 17 per cent were in precision production, craft, and repair positions' such as mechanics, welders and electricians (US Department of Labor, Bureau of Labor Statistics, 1992, p. 14). Accordingly, statistical analysis of earnings finds that individuals who qualified for their jobs by means of vocational education at the secondary level do not earn significantly more than individuals who reported that their jobs had no training requirement at all (Bowers and Swaim, 1992, table 7).

The question for evaluations of secondary vocational education, therefore, has not been whether graduates of these programs do better in the labor market than the general population. Instead, evaluations have focused on whether students in these programs experience more success than other high school students who do not go to college. Until the mid-1980s most studies of high school vocational education found no significant effect on students' subsequent employment or earnings, except for girls who studied office occupations (National Institute of Education, 1981; Psacharopoulos, 1987). These studies compared vocational graduates with other high school graduates who did not attend college, controlling for various measures of student background characteristics. The designation of vocational students often depended on self-descriptions by the students themselves.

However, in the mid-1980s researchers made two improvements. First, they used data from students' transcripts, instead of self-descriptions, to identify vocational students. Second, they discovered an important intervening variable: whether or not students became employed in the field for which they had trained. Using the NLSY data, Rumberger and Daymont (1984) found that boys who had studied trade and industry subjects, and girls who had studied for office occupations, faced significantly better prospects in the labor market after high school if they in fact found jobs in their fields of study.

Campbell, Elliot, Laughlin and Seusy (1987) replicated this result with HSB data. They found that vocational education participants who obtained a job in an occupation matching their field of training spent approximately 20 per cent more time in the labor market than a comparison group of general track students and their unemployment rate was three percentage points lower. In contrast, vocational participants who worked outside their field of training saw no advantage over the general track comparison group. High school students who concentrated in a particular vocational field and obtained related employment earned 7 to 8 per cent more than vocational students who found employment in unrelated fields or students who pursued a general program in high school. Vocational education participants who spent 100 per cent of their time working in related employment after graduation earned 31 per cent more than vocationally prepared students who took non-training related employment.

The importance of finding jobs related to field of training has also been demonstrated with secondary data from Hong Kong (Chung, 1990) and Israel (Neuman and Ziderman, 1991). Similar results with post-secondary data from the US are mentioned below. Along a similar line, Stevens (1993) has found that recent vocational graduates do best if they remain with the same employer for whom they worked while in school.

Still, even using these better methods, not all studies find positive effects of vocational education. Farkas, Hotchkiss and Stromsdorfer (1988) analyzed data from the second HSB follow-up, using the transcript classification scheme devised by Campbell *et al.* (1987) to define vocational concentrators. They found no effect of vocational education concentration, except for males who entered business and office jobs and for females who entered trade and industrial jobs. They concluded that there may be some training advantage for those pursuing jobs which are not traditional for their gender.

Given the evidence that placement in training-related jobs seems to improve the employment prospects of vocational graduates in the first few years after high school, it seems likely that the immediate pay-off from vocational education would be higher on average if more students did in fact obtain jobs related to their training. Yet Bishop (1989) notes that the proportion of vocational graduates who do find training-related placements ranges from a low of 17 per cent in some studies of trade and industrial graduates to a high of 52 per cent in some studies of health education graduates. He contrasts this with surveys finding that two-thirds of German apprentices obtained jobs related to their training.

If the only purpose of secondary vocational education were to improve students' employment and earnings immediately after high school, then these findings would imply that schools should try to design vocational education programs so as to increase the number of training-related placements. However, the purposes of secondary vocational education presumably also include promoting students' economic viability over the course of their working lifetimes, helping them find work that provides non-monetary satisfactions, and preparing them to be effective citizens as well as effective workers.

Campbell and Basinger (1985) studied some of these broader issues. They found that taking vocational courses or working in a training related job did not significantly affect students' subsequent job satisfaction. They also found that vocational students were less likely to participate in school organizations or non-school youth organizations than a comparable group of general track students. Controlling for social background and years of schooling, there were no differences in voting behavior, participation in political activity, or views of whether women should work.

Hotchkiss (1987) used HSB and NLSY data to examine four in-school outcomes — test scores, career expectations, grades, and attitudes — as well as five post high school outcomes: college attendance (two or four year), marriage and family, crime and substance use, and voting behavior. The effects of vocational curriculum on post high school outcomes appeared to be small and inconsistent. There is evidence of a tendency for vocational concentrators to use drugs less than general students. Hotchkiss found no important effects of vocational curriculum on voting behaviors. With regard to in-school outcomes, he found that participation in vocational education was not detrimental, but the absence of an academic curriculum was.

Altonji (1992) analyzed the effects of secondary school course-taking on students' subsequent education and labor market performance. Using the 1986 follow-up of the NLS72, he examined the effects of coursework in science, math, English, foreign language, social studies, fine arts, trades and industry, and business and marketing. An innovative statistical procedure was to use variation in course offerings among high schools to correct for bias resulting from students with unobserved differences choosing or being assigned to different courses. He found that students who took more vocational courses were earning higher wages fourteen years after graduation, but they also had finished fewer years of post-secondary education. This indicates that vocational programs in the early 1970s were preparing students for work but not for further education.

Conversely, Campbell *et al.* (1987) found that students who pursued an academic curriculum in high school but did not attend college earned less than those who pursued a general program. This indicates that academic studies prepared students for further education but not for work.

To summarize, high school vocational education has been found to be associated with higher earnings if students take a coherent sequence of courses and find jobs related to their training. Bishop (1994) believes the positive effects were greater in the 1980s than in the 1970s. However, only a small minority of high school students do complete a coherent sequence of vocational courses and then go on to related employment. Furthermore, students who take more vocational courses in high school also complete less further education beyond high school.

Altonji's is the first study that has tried to control for selection bias in measuring effects of secondary vocational education. Previous studies have not attempted to allow for the possibility that unmeasured characteristics of students affect both their likelihood of enrolling in vocational education and their subsequent performance in further education and the labor market. It is conceivable that some students are best suited for the kinds of work they can get with only a high school diploma, while others have a comparative advantage in more intellectual pursuits. Such pre-existing differences could explain the finding that vocational students do better in the labor market when they find jobs related to their training.

The possibility of pre-existing differences that make some young people naturally college-bound and others naturally work-bound has implications not only for research but also, more importantly, for policy. It would imply that it is most efficient to divide students into different kinds of programs according to their natural inclinations. However, there is no known empirical method that can reliably determine at, say, age 14 or 16, which students can potentially benefit most from further education. The most obvious indicator would be prior performance in school, but this is strongly correlated with socioeconomic and demographic variables, and disentangling these from the inclinations and talents of individual students is an empirically intractable task. Therefore current policy, as given in the 1990 Perkins Amendments and the 1994 School to Work Opportunities Act, seeks to keep the post-secondary option open for all students, through the integration of academic and vocational education. The next section examines evidence on the effectiveness of this approach.

Programs Integrating Academic and Vocational Education

The integration of academic and vocational education has been interpreted broadly by practitioners, researchers and policy makers. Grubb *et al.* (1990) have described eight models that capture the broad range of approaches that are being used in a variety of schools. The models range from beefing up the academic content of a single vocational course to occupational clusters and career academies that encompass a multi-year curriculum. Orr (1987) in a discussion of dropout prevention, advocates six different models that encourage the student's retention partially through integrated education and a connection to work. In 1988, the previous National Assessment of Vocational Education (NAVE) published a review of seven exemplary vocational education programs that describe a wide range of integrated curricula and educational approaches (Hayward *et al.* 1988).

The Southern Regional Education Board (SREB) promotes the integration of academic and vocational education in the context of workplace preparation. Student performance in eight of the original sites improved, with the greatest gains in the National Assessment of

Figure 4 :   Examples of programs integrating academic and vocational education

Program	Target population	Evaluation features
Principles of Technology Curriculum, AIT/CORD	Secondary students, ultimately at all levels of ability.	Multi-site evaluation, pre- and post-test assessments – comparison of means using paired t-test, coalition of expert educators on planning and design, case study analysis based on site observations.
Project COFFEE French River Education Group, North Oxford, Massachusetts	At-risk students from surrounding schools in region.	National Diffusion Network Evaluation Criteria, statistical comparison of completers to national norms, qualitative assessment.
Evaluation of Dropout Prevention and Re-entry Demonstration Projects in Vocational Education	Students at risk of dropping out of school, ten sites.	Two parts: (1) longitudinal study over three years with survey questionnaires and observations; and (2) control group model analyzing the impact of the educational programs – data collected from attendance, grades, credits. Three analytic techniques are used: analysis of covariance, 'reliability-corrected covariance analysis', and 'gap-reduction evaluation design'.
New York City's Career Magnet Schools	Students of all abilities, denoted by tested reading level.	Random assignment design using 'lottery' data on program/school selection, Analysis of Variance (ANOVA).
Career Academies	At-risk and other students	Matched comparison group in each site; benefit-cost analysis

Educational Progress made by those students who followed an integrated academic and vocational course of study (Harp, 1993). As of 1993, SREB was expanding this program to 300 sites.

Across the board, researchers and practitioners have commented on the incremental approach that integration takes as it is applied in the school site. Further, the variation of integration efforts also implies a range of evaluation methods. Figure 4 lists the programs that will be reviewed here, and summarizes the evaluation process that was used. Most of these programs began before the 1990 Perkins Amendments, but they nevertheless illustrate the integration of academic and vocational education as required by those Amendments.

Principles of Technology. This is an applied physics course developed by the Agency for Instructional Technology (AIT) and the Center for Occupational Research and Development (CORD). It has been widely adopted by teachers for integration efforts. AIT and CORD have evaluated the Principles of Technology program using a pre/post-test analysis during a pilot phase (AIT and CORD, 1984; AIT, 1986b), and case studies of schools where the courses have been added (AIT, 1986a). Stasz *et al.* (1993), have reported on this and other evaluations of CORD materials. In each of five studies, generally positive outcomes are reported although limitations in evaluation methods and research designs are noted.

For the pilot phase, the curriculum for the Principles of Technology course was divided into units, each of which underwent its own testing. In all cases, the tests were developed and refined by content experts at CORD. In addition, student attitude questionnaires and teacher questionnaires were distributed. The results distilled those areas of the curriculum with which students had the most difficulty, usually questions and manipulations using mathematics. Further, the structure of the test allowed for examination of progress based on gender, grade level, the class schedule and the specialty area of the instructor.

CORD has reported on the limitations of these evaluations. There is no matched control group in this study of students taking a similar course that is readily comparable to the Principles of Technology curriculum. The authors report that the administrative and fiscal costs involved in developing matched control groups would have been significant. But they also note that the matching process itself would have been difficult because of the composite academic and vocational approach in the Principles of Technology curriculum.

Another methodological issue is the use of the same test for pre- and post-test examinations, about one month apart. Although students were never given answers to the pre-test, they may have been sensitized by the questions to focus on certain concepts during the course. In addition, there was variation in laboratory equipment, teaching patterns and student characteristics. There has been no attempt to control for this variability.

The results showed that significant learning gains did occur and also identified areas where improvement might take place. These conclusions were drawn from the combined qualitative and quantitative assessments. Pre-test and post-test scores on the Principles of Technology Curriculum have been reported by CORD. The difference between the overall pre-test mean of 11.47 and the overall post-test mean of 24.4 was statistically significant at the .01 level using a paired t-test. Results for each curricular unit are listed in table 12.

In addition to the testing and the case studies that AIT and CORD use as evidence of their program's merits, it should also be noted that

Table 12: Principles of Technology, pre-test and post-test scores, units 1–10

Unit	Number of items	Pre-test mean (% correct)	Post-test Mean (% correct)
1	30	12.5 (41%)	20.1 (67%)
2	33	13.6 (41%)	17.6 (53%)
3	30	14.9 (49%)	19.4 (65%)
4	36	16.4 (46%)	24.4 (68%)
5	35	13.2 (38%)	22.6 (65%)
6	30	11.5 (38%)	18.3 (61%)
7	34	13.2 (39%)	19.9 (59%)
8	25	11.9 (48%)	18.9 (76%)
9	29	12.6 (33%)	22.1 (76%)
10	34	11.4 (34%)	24.4 (72%)

Source: Principles of Technology, Unit 10: Energy Converters, Pilot Test Findings, April 1986, p. 13.

the design of the CORD curriculum is also relevant. A consortium of thirty-three state and provincial education agencies from across the United States and Canada developed the curriculum that is used in Principles of Technology. Therefore, if we believe that expert opinion is relevant in the development of curricula that integrate academic and vocational skills, the development of this particular program appears to have drawn on a wide range of professional experience.

Even with this type of preparation, barriers to implementation still exist. Bodily *et al.* (1992), examined the use of CORD materials in selected school sites as part of an investigation of efforts to integrate academic and vocational curricula. In Ohio, for example, the State Department of Education encouraged schools to increase the teaching of applied academics and invested in CORD materials to this end. Teachers reported that the materials did not provide occupationally specific examples and that overall, the materials were too generic. Release time for teachers for the development of new packages as well as for the assimilation of these packages was recommended.

Project COFFEE. A comprehensive program for dropout prevention was designed by the Cooperative Federation for Educational Experiences (COFFEE) in North Oxford, Massachusetts in 1979 (see appendix A). Since its inception, the program has been widely replicated in other dropout prevention efforts and in vocational education for reentry students. Project COFFEE has undergone relatively rigorous scrutiny. It has been validated twice by the US Department of Education's Joint Dissemination Review Panel and is a demonstration program of the National Diffusion Network.

Project COFFEE is an integrated program that emphasizes academic and occupational development. Other significant features include

Table 13: *Means (and standard deviations) of California achievement test (CAT) scale score: pre, post and gains for COFFEE students in three years*

	Pre	Post	Gain
Year 1: 1982/1983, (M = 35, F = 12, N = 47)			
Reading	543.3 (60.3)	567.4 (76.9)	+24.1*
Language	526.7 (61.2)	553.6 (69.7)	+26.9*
Mathematics	514.7 (61.0)	538.8 (59.7)	+24.1*
Total	518.5 (64.0)	549.2 (64.1)	+30.7*
Year 2: 1983/1984, (M = 17, F = 3, N = 20)			
Reading	537.6 (62.3)	570.0 (76.5)	+32.4*
Language	514.2 (58.3)	538.2 (68.0)	+24.0*
Mathematics	507.8 (64.4)	526.5 (79.6)	+18.7
Total	514.1 (51.9)	534.9 (65.7)	+20.8*
Year 3: 1984/1985, (M = 27, F = 10, N = 37)			
Reading	521.8 (66.2)	546.6 (69.6)	+24.8*
Language	483.8 (74.1)	508.1 (66.3)	+24.3*
Mathematics	495.0 (60.9)	514.1 (64.2)	+19.1*
Total	490.1 (62.1)	526.1 (63.2)	+36.0*

Source: Project COFFEE, Submission Prepared for the Joint Dissemination Review Panel, 1986, pp. 26–8.
* $p < .05$

the use of full-time guidance counselors, an in-school suspension policy as a form of discipline, a pre-employment component to assist with job skills, and an active program in physical education. Occupational development relies heavily on simulated work experience in one of five training areas: computer maintenance, word processing, horticulture/agriculture, distributive education, building/grounds maintenance. Students also engage in job shadowing and internships. School-based enterprises are used to develop technical and interpersonal skills. All sectors of the Project COFFEE program are designed to support and reaffirm this occupational emphasis (French River Education Center, Inc., 1989).

Project COFFEE has been evaluated against three goals: first, gains in language, reading, and math will be greater than national norms; second, students will significantly lower their absentee rate; and third, they will have higher employability rates compared to those who had not attended the program. Assessment was accomplished by testing with the California Achievement Test, an ongoing review of attendance figures, and employment figures based on personal interviews, respectively. In all three cases, Project COFFEE has reported statistically significant gains (tables 13–16).

Table 14: *Percentage of COFFEE students increasing their percentile rankings from pre-to post-test*

	1982/1983	1983/1984	1984/1985
Reading	55.3	60.0	37.8
Language	55.3	65.0	47.4
Mathematics	62.2	65.0	51.4
Total	60.0	65.0	48.6

Table 15: *Mean (and standard deviation) of attendance: days present for COFFEE students before and during the program (maximum = 180 days)*

	1982/1983 N = 98	1983/1984 N = 28	1984/1985 N = 85
Year before COFFEE	121.8 (47.6)	149.8 (28.9)	146.4 (20.2)
Year during COFFEE	153.6 (21.0)	159.6 (20.2)	163.0 (15.3)
Differences	31.8*	9.8*	17.4*

* $p < .05$

Table 16: *Project COFFEE graduate employment/placement statistics**

	1980/1983[o]	1983/1984	1984/1985
Students served	165 (100%)	37 (100%)	24 (100%)
Students working[^]	81 (49%)	23 (62%)	17 (70%)
Military	18 (11%)	3 (8%)	0
Post-secondary education	12 (7%)	1 (3%)	2 (8%)
Students graduated	58 (35%)	20 (54%)	22 (92%)
Students mainstreamed	51 (31%)	5 (14%)	0
Students relocated	37 (22%)	4 (11%)	0
Student withdrawals	62 (38%)	12 (32%)	2 (8%)

* Columns add to more than 100 per cent because categories are not mutually exclusive.
[o] Cumulative graduate placement information has been included for 1980–83.
[^] This row is compared to US Department of Labor reports that 36 per cent of all white dropouts are employed (US Department of Labor, Employment and Training Report to the President, 1982).

The first and third claims are supported by comparisons to national norms. The second claim about attendance is a comparison over time of Project COFFEE students and does not include a national comparison group. To gauge improvement in language, reading, and math, Project COFFEE students were compared to a 'norm population chosen by McGraw-Hill to be representative of the typical high school students in the United States' (French River Education Center, Inc., 1989). The actual scores that are used for norm comparisons were not provided by Project COFFEE in their published report, but it does state, 'If COFFEE students were to maintain their relative standing with respect to the

test's norm population, students would have the same percentile rank-
ing on both pre and post tests. However, table 14 shows that a large
proportion of COFFEE students actually increase their percentile rankings
showing that they are outperforming the norms,' although in 1984/85
a majority of students did not improve their relative scores in three of
four subjects.

The claim that Project COFFEE students will have greater employment rates is supported by comparisons to national employment statistics for dropouts. As shown in table 16, the comparison of Project
COFFEE students working is made to US Department of Labor reports
showing 36 per cent of all white dropouts are employed.

In addition to the measurement of results from Project COFFEE,
the wide replication of the program is also evidence that practitioners
find the program design to be effective. Six of the ten projects chosen
for first year in-depth evaluation by the US Education Department's
Cooperative Demonstration Program, discussed next, were modeled
after Project COFFEE. (Hayward *et al.*, 1992).

*Dropout Prevention and Reentry Demonstration Projects in Voca-
tional Education* were funded by the Cooperative Demonstration Program of the Carl D. Perkins Act. Hayward *et al.* (1992) have prepared
the first of three years of longitudinal evaluation of the ten demonstration sites. The programs cover a wide range of target students, but all
integrate academic and vocational education as a central focus. Some
have close partnerships with business and apprenticeship programs as
well.

In assessing the effectiveness of the programs, two separate studies are being conducted. The first is a process evaluation that tries to
understand the issues involved in replicating a model program. The
second is an outcome evaluation to understand how students in these
programs perform compared to a control group at each site. Seven
used random assignment to form the control group. The three remain-
ing test sites used matched comparison groups.

The evaluation of outcomes used questionnaires and student records
to measure attitudes toward self and school, educational and occupational aspirations, academic performance, disciplinary events, attendance, dropout rates, and employability. Factor analysis identified five
attitudinal factors: attitude toward teachers/teaching, expectations for
the future, attitude toward counselors, perception of academic encour-
agement received, and sensitivity to classmates' disruptive behavior.

Three separate analytic techniques were used to estimate program
effects: regular analysis of covariance; 'reliability-corrected' covariance

analysis (used when the experimental and control groups were not randomly assigned); and a measure of the 'gap reduction' between students in the program and the school average.[1] In many instances these three methods gave different results. But in some sites, statistically significant changes were found indicating that students in the demonstration program were performing better than the control group. The authors note that significant changes were more often found in sites where the qualitative assessment of program implementation had also been favorable. The results are presented in table 17, showing which analytical techniques, if any, yielded statistically significant differences.

New York City's Career Magnet Program has been evaluated by random assignment, taking advantage of the lottery procedure that assigns ninth grade students to educational options (Crain, Heebner and Si, 1992). Career magnet programs are designed to combine academic and vocational education in order to make secondary education more relevant to the world of work, expand post-secondary education options, and enhance career-specific skills.

According to Crain *et al.* (*ibid.*), the experimental design met three criteria: (i) all students in the selection pool had the same likelihood of being admitted into the program; (ii) selection was random; and (iii) students who did participate in the career magnet program had a different educational program than the control group. While the structure of this evaluation is notable, the random assignment is part of the normal process of placing students in their high school program in New York City. Some students are selected for certain programs by certain schools through a complex quota system, but others are randomly assigned. Further, it is never clear to teachers, staff, or students whether a student is there as a result of the quota, or because the student was selected randomly. This protects against differential treatment of students in the school. The quota system is based mainly on reading ability and guarantees that students at each achievement level participate.

The evaluation had to take account of the range of programs from which students came, and the variety of magnet programs. Incomplete records kept some students from being included in the final analysis. Tables 18–20 show results of analysis of variance between pools of lottery 'winners' and lottery 'losers'. Table 18 shows outcomes for *all* career magnet programs in several types of schools, table 19 gives results for career magnet programs that exist only in total career magnet schools and table 20 shows results from career magnet programs that exist in comprehensive and vocational schools.

Tables 18–20 indicate that lottery winners are significantly more

Table 17: *Evaluation of dropout prevention and reentering demonstration projects in vocational education: summary of findings, school year 1989/90*

MEASURE	Arundel	Cushing	Oconce	Woods.	Portl.	Carlm.	Ft. B.	Ft. Y.	TM	Ft. T.
School performance										
Higher GPA	G	G		R,C,G		G				C,G
Higher number of credits earned		G		R,C	-R,-G					-R,-C
Fewer absences	C								R,C	
Fewer courses failed		G		G		C,G	-G			C,G
School affiliation										
School thought safer				R,C		R,C,G				
Teaching/teachers better		-G		R,C		R,C				
Discipline fairer				-G		G				
More school spirit		G	C			G			R,C	
Rules less strict		-G	G			R,C,G	-R			
Better job preparation			R			G	-R,-C			-R,-C
Counselling/counselors better		-R,-C	G							
More help choosing courses		-R,-C	G		C					
More academic encouragement			C,G			C	-G		-C	
Student perceptions that										
Classmates have diverse friendships	-G	-G		R,C		-R				G
Fewer classmates are critical						G				
Classmates should not misbehave							R,C			
Future expectations are better							-R		-R,-C	
Many classmates are college bound						G	C,G			

R = regular ANCOVA   C = reliability-corrected ANCOVA   G = gap reduction analysis; '-' = negative finding
Source: Hayward *et al.* (1992).

Table 18: Effect of career magnets on ninth grade student outcomes: analysis of variance of all career magnet programs

Outcomes	Students with 'average' reading scores (Wtd. N = 3272)			Students with 'below' or 'missing' reading scores (Wtd. N = 986)		
	Losers	Winners	Diff.	Losers	Winners	Diff.
% entering H.S.	86.00	89.00	+3.00°	77.00	83.00	+6.00*
% changing H.S.	15.00	14.00	−1.00	20.00	19.00	−1.00
% dropping H.S.	1.00	1.00	0.00	3.00	4.00	+1.00
% passing Regents math test	7.00	7.00	0.00	3.00	6.00	+3.00°
Increase in days absent since eighth grade	0.98	0.96	−0.20	0.62	1.75	+1.13°
Gain in DRP reading scores since eighth grade	3.19	4.61	+1.40°	4.35	3.04	−1.31
Credits earned net of pre-tests	3.88	4.18	+.30°	3.75	3.49	−0.26

Note: * = significant p < .10 (2-tailed)
° = significant p < .05 (2-tailed)
Source: Crain *et al.* (1992) table 8.

Table 19: Effect of career magnets on ninth grade student outcomes: analysis of variance in total career magnet programs

Outcomes	Students with 'average' reading scores (Wtd. N = 1864)			Students with 'below' or 'missing' reading scores (Wtd. N = 390)		
	Losers	Winners	Diff.	Losers	Winners	Diff.
% entering H.S.	89.00	91.00	+2.00	77.00	90.00	+13.00°
% changing H.S.	13.00	13.00	0.00	16.00	17.00	+1.00
% dropping H.S.	1.00	1.00	0.00	1.00	4.00	+3.00
% passing Regents math test	7.00	9.00	2.00	4.00	9.00	+5.00*
Increase in days absent since eighth grade	0.86	1.16	+0.30	0.58	1.92	+1.34*
Gain in DRP reading scores since eighth grade	3.50	4.41	+0.91	4.06	4.59	+0.53
Credits earned net of pre-tests	4.10	4.66	+0.56°	3.84	3.70	−0.14

Note: * = significant p < .10 (2-tailed)
ø = significant p < .05 (2-tailed)
Source: Crain *et al.* (1992) table 9.

likely to enter high school than lottery losers, though there is also an offsetting tendency, not quite significant statistically, for students who do win admission to career magnet school to dropout in larger numbers during ninth grade. Students with low reading scores prior to grade nine are more likely to pass the New York State Regents exam in math if they attend a career magnet school, despite the fact that the

Table 20: Effect of career magnets on ninth grade student outcomes: analysis of variance in comprehensive and vocational schools

Outcomes	Students with 'average' reading scores (Wtd. N = 1408)			Students with 'below' or 'missing' reading scores (Wtd. N = 596)		
	Losers	Winners	Diff.	Losers	Winners	Diff.
% entering H.S.	85.00	89.00	+4.00*	79.00	80.00	+1.00
% changing H.S.	17.00	14.00	–3.00	19.00	20.00	+1.00
% dropping H.S.	1.00	1.00	0.00	4.00	5.00	+1.00
% passing Regents math test	8.00	6.00	–2.00	3.00	4.00	+1.00
Increase in days absent since eighth grade	1.20	0.79	–0.41	0.65	1.67	+1.02ø
Gain in DRP reading scores since eighth grade	2.68	4.74	+2.06ø	4.56	2.00	–2.56
Credits earned net of pre-tests	3.60	3.60	0.00	3.68	3.34	–0.34

Note: * = significant p < .10 (2-tailed)
    ø = significant p < .05 (2-tailed)
Source: Crain *et al.* (1992) table 10.

magnet school students are also more likely to show an increase in absenteeism. Students with average reading scores before grade nine increase their reading scores as much as 50 per cent faster in career magnet schools than in regular schools. However, there is a tendency, though not statistically significant, for career magnet students with low initial reading scores to make less progress in reading than their counterparts in regular schools. On balance, the statistically significant results indicate that winning admission to a career magnet helps students with low initial reading scores to do better in math, students with high initial reading scores to do better in reading and both groups to stay in school for the start of ninth grade.

Career Academies in California started in 1981 enrolling students who, in ninth grade, had shown a combination of poor attendance, low grades and inadequate course completion by the end of their ninth grade. Patterned after the Philadelphia Academies which had started in the late 1960s, the California career academies are schools-within-schools for grades 10–12 that organize a complete high school curriculum around a career theme. Employers are involved as speakers, mentors, and providers of jobs for students during summer and part-time during the school year. The first two career academies in California, called the Peninsula Academies, focused on electronics and computer-related occupations. Subsequent academies have been organized around health careers, graphic arts, finance, and a number of other career themes (Stern, Raby and Dayton, 1992).

Table 21: Cumulative percentages of known and probable dropouts from California career academies and comparison groups, by cohort, as of Spring 1988

Cohort entrance date	Academy			Comparison group		
	Known drops	Probable drops	Total	Known drops	Probable drops	Total
Fall 1985 (543, 526)*	6.6%	0.7%	7.3%	11.0%	3.6%	14.6%
Fall 1986 (258, 448)	3.1%	3.5%	6.6%	10.3%	4.0%	14.3%
Fall 1987 (287, 441)	1.4%	1.4%	2.8%	2.0%	0.2%	2.2%

* Numbers in parenthesis are initial sizes of academy and comparison groups, respectively.
Source: Stern et al. (1989) pp. 410–1.

An evaluation was performed on ten sites that were funded by the State of California to replicate the Peninsula Academy model. There was a comparison group of non-academy students at each site, individually matched by gender, ethnicity, and performance in ninth grade, but students were not randomly assigned to the program and comparison groups. Results showed that in some, but not all, of the replication sites academy students had better attendance, higher grades, and a greater likelihood of staying in school (Stern *et al.*, 1988 and 1989). The gains for each cohort of academy students were greater during their first year than in subsequent years; this does not mean that the first-year gains were subsequently eroded, only that they were not augmented.

Table 21 shows the cumulative results of academy participation on school performance, as indicated by cumulative dropout rates for three cohorts of academy and comparison students. For those entering in fall 1985 (the only cohort the evaluation followed through grade 12), the higher graduation rate for academy students implies a social benefit that exceeds the incremental cost of the program (Stern *et al.*, 1989).

In summary, the integration of academic and vocational education has been applied to a range of students at different levels of achievement. Students in some of these integrated programs have done better than comparison groups in reading, math, attendance and persistence. While these positive school outcomes should contribute to students' career success, most of the evaluations reported here have not measured labor market outcomes. The exception is the evaluation of Project COFFEE, which did demonstrate a higher rate of employment among its graduates than among white high school dropouts nationwide. However, it would be useful to have more rigorous testing of the effects of integrated academic and vocational programs on students' actual transition to work.

Two-Year Colleges and Proprietary Schools

An increasing proportion of vocational and technical education is taking place in less-than-four-year post-secondary schools, both public and proprietary. Although federally supported vocational education is still limited to occupations not ordinarily requiring a bachelor's or advanced degree, the post-secondary schools prepare for a higher-paying segment of these occupations than secondary schools do. Nurses and various kinds of technicians are among the occupational groups in which large proportions of individuals report that they received their qualifying training in two-year colleges or proprietary schools (US Department of Labor, Bureau of Labor Statistics, 1992). Unlike those who qualified by means of secondary vocational programs, these post-secondary qualifiers obtain significantly higher earnings than individuals who report that their jobs required no special training at all (Bowers and Swaim, 1992).

Analytic Issues

To evaluate the effects of post-secondary education or training, it is necessary to take account of the fact that, unlike high school which is more or less compulsory, the decision to enroll in post-secondary education is voluntary. To inform policy, it is not enough to measure the difference in well-being between those who do and do not enroll. The question is whether individuals who do not (or who do) enroll would be better off if they did (or did not). For certain kinds of training programs, this can be answered by conducting an experiment in which individuals are randomly assigned to treatment and control groups. However, it is more difficult to conduct a random-assignment experiment to test the effects of attending a two-year college. Perhaps the nearest thing to a true experimental study on the effects of education is Angrist and Krueger's (1992) analysis of labor market outcomes for Vietnam-era young men whose participation in higher education was affected by the draft lottery. While their finding that ordinary non-experimental analysis apparently has not overstated the returns to schooling is of great interest, the pre-1992 Current Population Survey (CPS) data they were using does not permit specific analysis of non-baccalaureate post-secondary education. Consequently, inferences about the effects of two-year colleges or other post-secondary education must rely on naturally occurring variation in behavior.

Individual choices divide the population at several junctures. Some enter post-secondary education, some do not. Those who enter post-secondary education must choose among several kinds of institutions, and in most of these institutions they are given a choice of fields to study. Some hold paid jobs while in school, others do not. Some finish their programs, some do not. Some join the labor force after leaving school, others do not. Each of these choices may be affected by unmeasured variables which also affect subsequent economic success. If so, simply comparing economic outcomes for the sub-populations created at each choice point will not give an accurate measure of the true effect of each choice, even when observed differences among the sub-populations are taken into account.

Logically, self-selection can reflect either absolute or relative advantage (see Maddala, pp. 257–60). In comparing individuals who attend community college with others who do not participate in any post-secondary education, an absolute advantage for the community college group means that their economic performance would exceed that of the other group even if both groups had the same amount of schooling, be it community college or no post-secondary education. Relative advantage means that the high school group's performance would be better than the community college group's if neither group participated in post-secondary education, but the community college group would do better than the high school group if both groups attended community college. Absolute advantage entails a hierarchical ordering; relative advantage implies a more pluralistic pattern of rational self-selection (Willis and Rosen, 1979).

If community college students have an absolute advantage over individuals who possess only high school diplomas, then ordinary statistical procedures which do not take account of this advantage will overestimate the benefit of attending community college, by attributing to community college attendance differences that should properly be attributed to the prior advantage of those who attend. However, if the advantage of community college students is relative not absolute, then ordinary statistical procedures which fail to take account of it will actually underestimate the benefit of community college attendance. The reason is that standard procedures would assume that individuals who did not attend would have obtained the same benefit if they did attend, and would estimate that benefit as the difference in earnings (or other outcome) not attributable to other measured differences between attenders and non-attenders — but this contradicts the idea of relative advantage, which implies that non-attenders would not in fact obtain the same benefit if they did attend community college.

There have been some preliminary attempts to measure whether self-selection occurs in two-year colleges, and, if so, whether it reflects absolute or relative advantage. Grubb (1990) compared annual earnings of individuals who entered community colleges with those who completed high school only. He found evidence that men who entered community colleges had unobserved characteristics which correlated positively with earnings. However, the selection coefficients for females who entered community college were statistically insignificant, as were the selection coefficients for males or females who completed high school only. In sum, he found no clear pattern of self-selection.

Hollenbeck (1992) compared labor market outcomes of individuals who had participated in post-secondary technical education with those of others who had enrolled in academic post-secondary education with the intent of completing a baccalaureate. He found significant coefficients indicating an absolute advantage for the technical group. This surprising result may be attributable to the fact that the sample was the 1980 senior cohort from the High School and Beyond (HSB) survey, and the dependent variable was the logarithm of hourly wage in spring 1986, so that students who received baccalaureate degrees might not have had sufficient time to demonstrate their advantage in the labor market. Analysis of older cohorts will be necessary to establish whether selection effects are important.

Led by Heckman (1979), econometricians in the 1980s tried various procedures to correct for selection bias. However, when applied to training programs, these procedures yielded results which were very sensitive to assumptions about unobserved variables, and which differed from results obtained by actual controlled experimentation (LaLonde, 1986). This led many to conclude that experiments with random assignment were necessary.

While random assignment of individuals to treatment and control groups does eliminate the influence of unmeasured variables in large samples, it also can create other problems. Unlike medical research, evaluations of education and training programs cannot administer a placebo. Therefore, individuals who are turned away from a program may feel some disappointment, after they have decided they wanted to participate and have made the commitment of applying. This may have a discouraging effect on their subsequent behavior. The result would be worse performance by individuals in the control group than if they had never heard about the program. This may explain why losers in the lottery for admission to New York City career magnet high schools were less likely to show up for ninth grade (see tables 16–18 above). The existence of such a 'disappointment effect' would tend to bias the evaluation in favor of finding positive results for the treatment group.

Another analytic issue has to do with how educational attainment is specified. In the varied world of post-secondary education, individuals may acquire certificates and degrees in various combinations. Perhaps it matters whether someone who obtains a baccalaureate, for example, has also picked up an associate degree along the way. Unfortunately, most of the empirical work on returns to post-secondary education has simply classified individuals according to their highest educational attainment. Hollenbeck (1992) is an exception: he includes an indicator of whether individuals have received a vocational certificate or degree prior to obtaining a baccalaureate. The association of this indicator with wages and earnings is often statistically significant, but its sign is sometimes positive and sometimes negative.

A conventional way to measure the payoff from education or training is to compute the internal rate of return, defined as the value of the discount rate that equates the present value of costs and benefits. The private economic benefits from investing in education or training include increased earnings and consumption benefits. Social benefits include these plus any externalities. Private costs include tuition and other out-of-pocket expenses, plus earnings foregone while attending school. For post-secondary students, foregone earnings are a major component of cost. Social costs also include any public subsidies.

Mincer (1974) introduced a technique for estimating the private rate of return to schooling directly from a regression in which the logarithm of earnings is a linear function of years of schooling and other predictors. The coefficient on years of schooling is an estimate of the rate of return. This technique has become widely used, but its derivation is sometimes forgotten. In Mincer's derivation it is assumed that each year of schooling is a year of foregone earnings. (In this tradition, out-of-pocket expenses are sometimes assumed to be paid from earnings during the summer, when school is not in session.) That is, work life begins when schooling ends.

This assumption no longer fits the facts for post-secondary students, however. CPS data reveal that 45 per cent of college students were employed in 1959, and 56 per cent in 1986. Among 21-year-old college students in the National Longitudinal Survey of Youth Labor Market Experience (NLSY), employment rose from 52 per cent in the spring of 1979 to 63 per cent in spring, 1986. The NLSY data show employment rates are slightly higher among two-year than among four-year college students (Stern and Nakata, 1991). Many two-year colleges have accommodated working students by scheduling more classes at night.

Since a year of post-secondary schooling can no longer be

considered a year of foregone earnings, the coefficient on years of schooling in a regression for the logarithm of earnings can no longer be interpreted as a rate of return. It simply measures the percentage increase in earnings associated with an additional year of schooling. Computing the rate of return to schooling requires comparing this benefit with the cost of schooling, which must be measured directly.

Unfortunately, there do not seem to be any studies on the actual amount of foregone earnings while in college. Existing longitudinal surveys contain enough information to estimate foregone earnings with reasonable accuracy, but no one appears to have done this analysis yet. The findings from such an analysis could have decisive implications for the rate of return. For instance, Stern and Nakata (*ibid.*) found that the rate of return to two years of college for a male whose annual college expenses were $3000 would be 14.1 per cent if he earned $1500 a year while in college, but if he earned $7500 a year as a student the rate of return would be 29.6 per cent.

Freeman (1974) recognized the importance of this issue in his analysis of the economic pay-off from training in proprietary business colleges and technical institutes. He observed that these schools made special efforts to reduce the opportunity cost of students' time by scheduling classes in the evening or in concentrated blocks during the morning or afternoon. As a result, a year of instruction in proprietary schools cost less than a year of college in foregone work hours. Using data on average work hours for students in proprietary schools and colleges, Freeman converted the actual time and money cost of schooling into year-equivalents. He used this to adjust the rate of return to schooling, estimated from a regression equation of the logarithm of earnings on reported years of schooling. The adjusted estimate represents a rate of return per true year-equivalent invested in schooling.

In addition to complicating the estimation of the rate of return to schooling, the fact that many students are employed while in school also raises other issues. One is, which comes first? Standard procedures for estimating the economic outcomes of schooling are still formulated as if students go first to school, then to work. In fact, however, many young people spend several years after high school drifting from one job to another, as we have already pointed out, while at the same time dropping into and out of post-secondary education. At some point a definable career interest may eventually start to gel. An actual work experience may be the precipitating factor in forming this stable identification with a particular line of work or a particular employer. Having identified desirable work, it may then become necessary to return to school in order to fill in missing qualifications or become eligible for advancement. Work experience may therefore precede schooling in preparing for eventual long-term employment. If so, work experience prior to and during the course of schooling may affect post-school success differently than work experience after schooling has been completed.

Some indication that work experience during high school affects subsequent career success has come from studies of employed students reviewed in Chapter 2. With regard to employment of post-secondary students, Stephenson (1981 and 1982) analyzed data from the National Longitudinal Survey of Young Men and found that employment during college was positively related to wages a few years afterward. Stephenson treated work experience as exogenous, ignoring the possibility that employment during college and subsequent success in the labor market might both result, at least in part, from other variables such as ability or ambition. However, San (1986), using the same data set, also found that work during college was positively associated with earnings a few years later, even allowing for work during college to be endogenous. As mentioned in Chapter 2, this is consistent with findings for high school students: namely, a positive correlation between time spent working while in school and subsequent employment or earnings (Meyer and Wise, 1982; d'Amico, 1984; Bishop, Blakemore and Low, 1985; Mortimer and Finch, 1986; Stern and Nakata, 1989; Ruhm, 1993).

While these results point to the possibility that work and school may interact positively to influence subsequent career success, there is also evidence that working while in college increases the probability of dropping out (Kohen, Nestel and Karmas, 1978; Ehrenberg and Sherman, 1987). Consistent with Astin (1975), Ehrenberg and Sherman find this effect is smaller if students are working on campus, perhaps because their work is related to what they are studying, or because on-campus jobs are more likely to accommodate students' schedules. The relatedness of school and work may be important not only in reducing the degree to which work interferes with school, but also in producing positive effects later.

National Data Sources

Several national data sets include information on economic returns to non-baccalaureate education and training. The decennial US Census of Population and Housing has the most complete coverage of the population. For the first time in 1990 the census question on educational attainment began to distinguish between completion of a two-year associate degree and completion of some college but no degree. Previously, census data did not distinguish between these two levels of schooling. Furthermore, holders of two-year degrees are asked if they are academic or vocational. Analysis of 1990 census data will therefore permit the most detailed analysis of earnings and other payoffs to a two-year degree within various demographic groups. However, the decennial census has two major drawbacks: it occurs only every ten years, and it is not longitudinal.

Two other surveys, both also conducted by the Census Bureau, partially compensate for these shortcomings of the decennial census. The Current Population Survey (CPS) draws a random sample of civilian, non-institutional households each month. About 60,000 households are currently targeted for the monthly survey, but about 2600 of these are not available for interviews (US Bureau of the Census, 1992, p. D-1). The March CPS survey includes detailed questions about income, which permit comparisons of earnings by educational attainment. The Survey of Income and Program Participation (SIPP) is another sample survey of households, focusing on labor force status, earnings and participation in government transfer programs. The SIPP and CPS samples are structured as short-term panels, with data collected on each individual for about two years. SIPP panels were started in 1984, 1986 and 1987. The 1987 panel included 33,100 eligible individuals, of whom 24,400 were interviewed for the life of the panel (*ibid.*, p. D-2). Because they include more detailed questions on education, training and employment, the CPS and SIPP permit more thorough cross-sectional studies. The CPS is also useful for measuring aggregate year-to-year trends. However, none of these surveys provides long-term longitudinal data.

The first survey that provides data for estimating the long-term consequences of non-baccalaureate education, including specifically participation in two-year colleges, is the National Longitudinal Study of the High School Class of 1972 (NLS72), sponsored by the US Department of Education. The original sample consisted of 22,652 randomly selected seniors within a stratified probability sample of US high schools. Following the baseline survey in spring, 1972, the sample has been resurveyed by mail in 1973, 1974, 1976, 1979 and 1986. The NLS72 have been used to analyze economic returns to non-baccalaureate education and training by Grubb (1991b and 1992a), Hollenbeck (1992) and Kane and Rouse (1992).

Another longitudinal survey sponsored by the US Department of Education is High School and Beyond (HSB). Designed to study both progress through high school and subsequent behavior, HSB started in spring 1980 with a sample of 30,030 high school sophomores and

28,240 seniors, randomly selected within a stratified probability sample of US high schools. Follow-ups have occurred in 1982, 1984 and 1986. Economic returns to non-baccalaureate education and training in the HSB data have been studied by Horn (1989); Lyke, Gabe and Aleman, 1991; and Hollenbeck (1992).

The National Longitudinal Survey of Youth Labor Market Experience (NLSY) is the latest of five cohorts comprising the National Longitudinal Surveys. The earlier cohorts included older and younger men and women. The surveys have all been conducted by the Center for Human Resources Research at Ohio State University, under contract with the US Department of Labor. NLSY began in 1979 with 14 to 21-year-olds and has followed them through 1988. The base year national probability sample included 11,406 civilian respondents and 1280 youth in the military. Information on labor market experience and further education have been collected annually. Transcript data for about 77 per cent of the civilian respondents have also been collected. A separate file contains week-by-week work histories. Monk-Turner (1986) analyzed returns to two-year college attendance among the NLS young men and young women. The NLSY cohort has now matured to the point where it would be worth analyzing the effects of non-baccalaureate, post-secondary education and training, and several investigators are now working on this, but no results have yet been published or presented at this time.

The Panel Study of Income Dynamics (PSID) is the longest-lived continuous survey of a nationally representative sample. Maintained by the Institute for Social Research at the University of Michigan, it was originally called the Survey of Economic Opportunity when it began in 1966 to assess the impact of anti-poverty programs. Subsequently it was expanded into a longitudinal study of economic well-being. The 1968 study was based on a nationally representative sample of 4802 households in forty states. The study has followed the original households as well as the 'split-offs' who left home to establish new households. Detailed employment and educational histories have been collected for new household heads and wives over the years, and for all heads and wives in 1976 and 1985. There are both household-level and individual-level longitudinal files available for public use.

There is continued interest in using individual earning records that are collected for administrative purposes to analyze the effects of participation in educational programs that cannot be evaluated experimentally. Stevens (1991) has described the possible use of unemployment insurance (UI) earnings data for this purpose. Since 1988 employers in all states have been required to make quarterly wage reports on individuals covered by UI. Social Security numbers can be used to link individuals' reported earnings to their school records in states where the school systems keep Social Security numbers in students' files. At least ten states have used UI data to evaluate vocational education programs. One major drawback of the UI data is that they exclude some workers: self-employed and federal employees, among others. Another major problem is that the records are kept by each state's employment security agency, so that an individual who goes to school in one state but then goes to work in another state would not have a complete school-and-work record in either state. This latter problem could conceivably be rectified by assembling state files at the national level. Since UI records already exist, it is worth the effort to try to solve these and other problems, or try to work around them. Stevens (1992) reports some early findings that illustrate what might be learned from UI data.

The National Center on the Educational Quality of the Workforce (1992) has produced a crosswalk that compares questions on education and training for the CPS, SIPP, NLS72, NLSY and HSB surveys. In addition to showing the specific wording of each question, the crosswalk also provides information about skip patterns, demographic questions, and sample characteristics.

Results for Two-Year Colleges

Cross-sectional differences in earnings between graduates of two-year colleges and graduates of high school only are available for all age groups from the Survey of Income and Program Participation (SIPP). Average monthly earnings over a four-month period were reported in spring 1987 (Kominski, 1990, table 2). Multiplying these by twelve gives the following estimated increments in annual earnings for holders of associate degrees compared to high school graduates:

age 25–34	$5016
35–44	7068
45–54	6528
55–64	3852

More recent estimates are available from the Current Population Survey (CPS). In 1992 the CPS began using the new Census question on educational attainment. The March, 1992 survey (US Bureau of the Census, 1992) found the following differences in mean 1991 earnings between individuals with associate degrees and individuals with only high school diplomas (or equivalent):

	Male				**Female**			
Age	**All**	**White**	**Black**	**Hispanic**	**All**	**White**	**Black**	**Hispanic**
25–34	$4912	4576	5644	4520	5346	5518	3589	5355
35–44	9007	8792	9590	8656	6485	6279	5403	NA
45–54	7974	8595	NA	NA	4696	4362	8198	NA
55–64	1028	1013	NA	NA	7540	7824	NA	NA

The first thing to note about these differences is that they are substantial, ranging from $3589 among 25–34-year-old black women to $9590 for 35–44-year-old black men. The extra earnings for men with an associate degree first increase, then decrease with age. This suggests that the degree opens additional opportunities for advancement through mid-career. The later decline may reflect either obsolescence of knowledge represented by the degree, or perhaps a vintage effect, if men who were 55–64-years-old in 1992 obtained their associate degrees at an earlier time and if the quality of degree programs used to be lower. However, the earnings advantage for 55–64-year-old women with associate degrees is greater than for any other age group. Explaining these divergent patterns will be an interesting challenge for future research. Part of the explanation may have to do with differences between vocational and academic associate degrees: the CPS question distinguishes between the two, but the published tables, from which the numbers above were taken, do not.

Of course these differences in earnings may reflect prior differences between associate degree recipients and high school graduates, rather than the effect of the associate degree itself. For instance, individuals who obtain associate degrees tend to come from more educated or affluent families than those who complete high school only (Lyke, Gabe and Aleman, 1991, table B.3). They also possess more of certain abilities, measured by grades and test scores (*ibid.*, tables B.4 and B.5), which lead to both higher educational attainment and higher earnings. And there are differences in gender, ethnic composition, and amount of work experience. To obtain a more precise measure of the economic pay-off from an associate degree, it is necessary to control statistically for these variables.

Such statistical control is possible with the detailed data from longitudinal data sets such as the High School and Beyond (HSB) survey and the National Longitudinal Study of the High School Class of 1972

Table 22.1: Point estimates of increment in annual earnings resulting from two-year college, compared to high school graduates

	Increase in current wage × 2000		Increase in annual earnings	
	Experience not controlled	Experience controlled	Experience not controlled	Experience controlled
Males[a]				
Vocational AA	–520		975	
Academic AA	–1,382		–1927	
Certificate	–286		–1801	
Credits for Non-degree Completers ($ per credit)				
Vocational	80		89	
Academic	–20		5	
Females[b]				
Vocational AA	3020		2723	
Academic AA	272		572	
Certificate	464		608	
Credits for Non-degree Completers ($ per credit)				
Vocational	–46		–8	
Academic	96		46	

[a] NLS72 data, 1986 Wages, 1985 Earnings; n = 3155 for wages, 3316 for earnings
[b] NLS72 data, 1986 Wages, 1985 Earnings; n = 2899 for wages, 3086 for earnings
Source: Grubb (1993b) table 1.

(NLS72). The HSB cohort of seniors in 1980 were resurveyed in 1986, when most of them were around age 24. Most of those who went to two-year colleges would have finished or dropped out by then. The 1986 HSB senior follow-up therefore provides good information for assessing the short-term pay-off from two-year college attendance. The NLS72 cohort was also resurveyed in 1986, when most of them were around age 32. This provides good information on respondents a little further on in their careers.

Results from several studies of these and other longitudinal data sets are summarized in tables 22.1–22.6, which report the incremental yearly earnings associated with two-year college attendance. The differences shown are either in reported earnings for a given year, or in hourly wages multiplied by 2000 to convert them into an annual estimate. All the differences shown in tables 22.1–22.6 are estimated from regression equations which include controls for demographic variables, socioeconomic background, and measured ability. Where indicated, the regressions also control for amount of work experience.

The HSB data were analyzed by Horn (reported in Goodwin, 1989),

Table 22.2: Point estimates of increment in annual earnings resulting from two-year college, compared to high school graduates

	Increase in current wage × 2000		Increase in annual earnings	
	Experience not controlled	Experience controlled	Experience not controlled	Experience controlled
Males and Females Pooled				
HSB Senior Cohort[a]				
Attended 24 months, obtained voc certificate or degree, had 80 per cent of credits in voc	1757		309	
Attended 6 months, no certificate or degree, had 20 per cent of credits in voc	1757		2296	
NLS72 Data[b]				
Attended 24 months, obtained voc certificate or degree, had 80 per cent of credits in voc	2341		2174	
Attended 6 months, no certificate or degree, had 20 per cent of credits in voc	-18		913	

[a] 1986 wages, 1985 earnings. Effects computed at reported mean wage $7.32, earnings $12,266. Table 5; n = 4460 for wages, 5964 for earnings
[b] 1986 wages, 1985 earnings. Effects computed at reported mean wage $10.94, earnings $21,741. Table 6; n = 4697 for wages, 5357 for earnings
Source: Hollenbeck (1992).

Table 22.3: Point estimates of increment in annual earnings resulting from two-year college, compared to high school graduates

	Increase in current wage × 2000		Increase in annual earnings	
	Experience not controlled	Experience controlled	Experience not controlled	Experience controlled
Males and Females Pooled				
HSB Senior Cohort[a]				
Completed two years (60 credits) of vocational coursework	3255			

[a] 1986 Data
Source: Horn (chapter 5, table 5.1, in Goodwin, 1989).

Table 22.4: Point estimates of increment in annual earnings resulting from two-year college, compared to high school graduates

		Increase in current wage × 2000		Increase in annual earnings	
		Experience not controlled	Experience controlled	Experience not controlled	Experience controlled
Males[a]					
	Vocational AA	524			
	Math-science AA[c]	3608			
	Other AA	480			
	Missing AA type	2814			
	Courses for non-degree completers ($ per course)			1129	
Females[b]					
	Vocational AA	4900			
	Math-science AA[c]	2000			
	Other AA	1522			
	Missing AA type	4418			
	Courses for non-degree completers ($ per course)			738	

[a] NLS72 data, 1986 Wages, effects on wages computed at mean $9.02 (reported in Grubb, 1992b, appendix A.).
[b] NLS72 data, 1986 Wages, effects on wages computed at mean $7.47 (reported in Grubb, 1992b, appendix A.).
[c] Includes engineering.
Source: Kane and Rouse (1992).

Table 22.5: Point estimates of increment in annual earnings resulting from two-year college, compared to high school graduates

		Increase in current wage × 2000		Increase in annual earnings	
		Experience not controlled	Experience controlled	Experience not controlled	Experience controlled
Males[a]					
	Completed community or junior college	−902			
Females[b]					
	Completed community or junior college	216			

[a] HSB cohort of 1980 seniors, wages in January 1986. Table B.17, n = 3425.
[b] HSB cohort of 1980 seniors, wages in January 1986. Table B.17, n = 3051.
Source: Lyke, Gabe, and Aleman (1991).

Table 22.6: *Point estimates of increment in annual earnings resulting from two-year college, compared to high school graduates*

	Increase in current wage × 2000		Increase in annual earnings	
	Experience not controlled	Experience controlled	Experience not controlled	Experience controlled
Males and Females Pooled[a]				
Started in community college and completed two years of schooling (may have transferred to four-year college)	624			

[a] NLS Young Men and Young Women in 1968, 10 years after high school. Effect computed at mean wage $2.89 for community college entrants. Table 3, n = 269.
Source: Monk-Turner (1986).

Hollenbeck (1992) and by Lyke, Gabe, and Aleman (1991). Horn's results imply a yearly earnings advantage of roughly $3000 for those who complete a two-year vocational program, compared to those who complete high school only. Horn's calculation assumes each year's course work includes thirty credits that are in the same field as respondents' subsequent employment. Hollenbeck's estimate for a vocational completer who attended for twenty-four months is about $1800. On the other hand, Lyke, Gabe and Aleman find an insignificant difference between community college and high school graduates, where the type of associate degree (academic versus vocational) is not taken into account. Differences in specification among the three analyses make it difficult to see exactly why these findings vary, but it appears that the early payoff from a vocational associate degree is greater than from an academic degree.

The NLS72 data have been studied by Grubb (1992a and 1993b), Hollenbeck (1992) and by Kane and Rouse (1992). Grubb found a vocational associate degree is worth in the vicinity of $3000 a year for females, but does not contribute much to additional earnings for males. These estimates are in the same ballpark as Hollenbeck's finding of a $2000 advantage for those who attended community college and received vocational certificates or degrees; Hollenbeck did not report separate analyses for males and females. Kane and Rouse found additional earnings of almost $5000 for females who obtained vocational associate degrees. The increment for males with vocational associate degrees was only one-tenth as big.

Medrich and Vergun (1994) found that women, but not men, who were employed full-time received an additional boost in annual pay if they were working in a job that was related to their vocational field of study. This analysis looked at earnings from 1990 to 1992 for 18–34-year-old SIPP respondents who attained a post-secondary degree in a vocational field no later than fall, 1990. The result for females is similar to results for high school vocational graduates described earlier.

In the NLS72 data, Grubb (1992a and 1993b) and Kane and Rouse (1992) also estimated the financial return to associate degrees in non-vocational fields. They found little or no gain in earnings for men or women, except for those with associate degrees in math or science.

As expected, all of these estimates of earnings differences for two-year college graduates, controlling for ability and demographic characteristics, are less than the simple, uncontrolled differences observed in the SIPP and CPS data.

Since most students who enter two-year colleges do not complete associate degrees, it is important to estimate the payoff from taking courses and not finishing the degree. As shown in tables 22.1, 22.2 and 22.4, estimates vary. Grubb finds little effect of credits for non-completers. Hollenbeck finds little effect on wages but a substantial effect on hourly earnings in the NLS72 data. He also finds large pay-offs for non-completers in the HSB data. Kane and Rouse find a positive wage pay-off for non-completers in the NLS72 data. It is hard to know what to make of these divergent results. Grubb (1993b) warns that the variety of programs and local circumstances makes it hazardous to generalize about effects.

Results for Proprietary Vocational Schools

SIPP data show the following differences between individuals who hold a post-secondary vocational certificate (including proprietary schools) and those who graduated from high school only (Kominski, 1990, table 2):

age 25–34	$636
35–44	1728
45–54	3900
55–64	6360

These differences increase substantially with age. This suggests some kind of complementarity between proprietary school training and work experience. It may be that individuals with vocational certificates are able to obtain more on-the-job training, or to make better use of it. It may also be that individuals tend to enroll in proprietary vocational schools after they have had enough successful work experience to see

Table 23.1: *Point estimates of increment in annual earnings resulting from proprietary vocational schools, compared to high school graduates*

		Increase in current wage × 2000		Increase in annual earnings	
		Experience not controlled	Experience controlled	Experience not controlled	Experience controlled
Males[a]					
	Certificate	1320	2062		
	Credits for non-completers ($ per credit)	20	–203		
Females[b]					
	Certificate	2680	698		
	Credits for non-completers ($ per credit)	20	96		

[a] NLS72 data, 1986 wages, 1985 earnings, table 7.
[b] NLS72 data, 1986 wages, 1985 earnings, table 8.
Source: Grubb (1991b).

Table 23.2: *Point estimates of increment in annual earnings resulting from proprietary vocational schools, compared to high school graduates*

	Increase in current wage × 2000		Increase in annual earnings	
	Experience not controlled	Experience controlled	Experience not controlled	Experience controlled
Males and Females Pooled				
HSB Senior Cohort[a]				
Attended 12 months, obtained voc certificate or degree, had all credits in voc		2108		1864

[a] 1986 wages, 1985 earnings. Effects computed at reported mean wage $7.32, earnings $12,266. Table 5; n = 4460 for wages, 5964 for earnings
Source: Hollenbeck (1992).

how they can benefit from this training. Another conceivable explanation is that older workers attended proprietary schools in an earlier time, when these schools may have offered programs of higher quality than in more recent years.

Tables 23.1–23.4 show results of studies using the HSB and NLS72 data to control for individual ability and demographic characteristics in estimating the pay-off to proprietary school training. In the short-term data from HSB, Lyke and associates find proprietary school graduates make about $1000 a year more than high school graduates. This is

Table 23.3: Point estimates of increment in annual earnings resulting from proprietary vocational schools, compared to high school graduates

	Increase in current wage × 2000		Increase in annual earnings	
	Experience not controlled	Experience controlled	Experience not controlled	Experience controlled
Males[a]				
Vocational School degree	1548			
Females[b]				
Vocational School degree	2083			

[a] NLS72 data, 1986 Wages, effects on wages computed at mean $9.02. Table 3a, n = 2476.
[b] NLS72 data, 1986 Wages, effects on wages computed at mean $7.47. Table 4a, n = 2751.
Source: Kane and Rouse (1992).

Table 23.4: Point estimates of increment in annual earnings resulting from proprietary vocational schools, compared to high school graduates

	Increase in current wage × 2000		Increase in annual earnings	
	Experience not controlled	Experience controlled	Experience not controlled	Experience controlled
Males[a]				
Completed Proprietary	1066			
Proprietary Non-completers	857			
Females[b]				
Completed Proprietary	1434			
Proprietary Non-completers	561			

[a] HSB cohort of 1980 seniors, wages in January 1986. Table B.17, n = 3425.
[b] HSB cohort of 1980 seniors, wages in January 1986. Table B.17, n = 3051.
Source: Lyke, Gabe and Aleman (1991).

more than the earnings advantage they found for individuals with associate degrees (academic and vocational together). Hollenbeck estimated a pay-off of approximately $2000 a year from a year in proprietary school — again somewhat more than his own estimate of the payoff from a community college vocational certificate or degree.

In the NLS72 data, with a somewhat older group, the estimates by Grubb and by Kane and Rouse show an earnings gain of $1000 to $2000 for proprietary school graduates. For non-completers, Grubb finds no significant pay-off. This is a perceptibly smaller pay-off than these investigators found for community college vocational graduates. Comparing the NLS72 and HSB estimates does not replicate the rising pay-off among older individuals as found in the SIPP data.

Summary

The results for two-year colleges and proprietary schools can be briefly summarized as follows:

Attendance at a two-year college is associated with substantially higher earnings for females who complete associate degrees, especially in vocational fields. There is not much evidence of a financial return to associate degrees for males, except possibly in math and science. Evidence on the returns for non-completers is mixed. CPS data show the 1991 earnings advantage of associate degree holders over high school graduates with no post-secondary education was in the range of $1000 to $9000 when no adjustment is made for differences in family background or prior achievement in school. The unadjusted difference is highest in the 35–44 age group for men, 55–64 for women. However, when prior differences are statistically controlled, using longitudinal data from the NLS72 and HSB surveys, studies find a 1985 earnings advantage in the range of $500 to $5000 at age 24 to 32 for associate degree holders compared to high school graduates.

Attendance at a proprietary vocational or technical school is also associated with gains in earnings. Unadjusted for prior differences, the annual earnings advantage for proprietary school attendees over high school graduates with no post-secondary education is in the range of $1000 to $6000, according to 1987 SIPP data, which also show the greatest difference at age 55–64. When differences in family background and prior school achievement are statistically controlled, the estimated 1985 earnings advantage of proprietary school graduates over high school graduates is usually estimated to be $1000 to $2000 at age 24 to 32. Studies using HSB data have found a slightly bigger advantage for proprietary graduates than for two-year degree holders around age 24, but studies using NLS72 data have found the opposite result around age 32.

Bigger earning gains do not necessarily imply that one program is more socially profitable than another. Different education and training programs serve different clienteles. They also have different costs, and different divisions of cost between public and private. Definitive judgment of the relative efficiency of different programs would require, first, that the programs be applied to similar populations or, if this is not possible, that differences among the participants in different programs be statistically controlled. Second, costs should be accurately measured. Unfortunately, not enough attention has been given to measuring costs, in particular the opportunity cost of foregone earnings for participants in education or training programs. Further analysis of existing data from longitudinal studies could yield valuable information about this.

Existing longitudinal studies should also keep following their samples as they age. One reason is to resolve the puzzling age pattern of earnings differences associated with two-year colleges and proprietary schools that appears in cross-sectional data. Cross-sectional differences are biggest after age 35 for male graduates of two-year college, and after age 55 for proprietary school attendees and female graduates of two-year colleges. But existing longitudinal data sets that include the period when most individuals attended these schools have so far followed them only to age 32 (NLS72), age 24 (HSB) or age 30 (NLSY).

Tech-prep: Bridging Secondary and Post-secondary

The tech-prep initiative aims to develop articulated programs that offer four years of sequential coursework intended to provide training for specific technical careers. These begin in the last two years of high school, are completed after two years of post-secondary training, and lead to an associate degree in such fields as business, health, engineering and agriculture. Furthermore, unlike previous efforts, the federal government has offered direct support by enacting the Tech-prep Education Act as part of the 1990 amendments to the Perkins Act, and allocating over $63 million in FY1991 and $90 million in FY1992 to promote the development and operation of articulated 2 plus 2 tech-prep initiatives.

Essential Features of Tech-prep

In *The Neglected Majority* (1985), Dale Parnell, then the Executive Director of the American Association of Community and Junior Colleges, offered a potential option for bringing technical education into the mix of educational reform. This book brought widespread attention to the concept of tech-prep. Parnell argued for a complete restructuring of general education curricula. According to Parnell, the content of tech-prep should be a foundation of basic proficiency development in math, science, communications, and technology in an applied setting. He further recommended substantive program coordination between secondary and post-secondary schools. With this framework as a guide, tech-prep-type initiatives began developing across the country in the late 1980s.

The educational strategy selected by the Congress for the Tech-prep Education Act of 1990 was quite similar to those outlined in the secondary and post-secondary portions of *The Neglected Majority*. Tech-prep education was defined as:

> . . . a combined secondary and post-secondary program which:
> (A) leads to a two-year associate degree or a two year certificate;
> (B) provides technical preparation in at least one field of engineering technology, applied science, mechanical, industrial, or practical art, or trade, or agriculture, health, or business;
> (C) builds student competence in mathematics, science, and communications (including through applied academics) through a sequential course of study; and
> (D) leads to placement in employment. (The Tech-prep Education Act of 1990, p. 40)

In developing regulations for the implementation of the Tech-prep Education Act, the United States Department of Education accordingly specified desirable components by awarding preference points to projects which:

- provide for effective employment placement activities or transfer of students to four-year baccalaureate programs;
- are developed in consultation with business, industry and labor unions;
- address effectively the issues of dropout prevention and re-entry and the needs of minority youth of limited English proficiency, youth with handicaps, and disadvantaged youth.

The principal defining characteristic of tech-prep is curriculum articulation. Tech-prep represents an advance over prior articulation efforts in that the articulation occurs between programs or majors (for example, health, graphic arts, etc.) and is not limited merely to courses (for example, welding, shorthand).

Earlier efforts at articulation (including most 2 plus 2 programs) made little or no attempt to integrate the vocational and academic curriculum at either the high school or community college level. Although many tech-prep programs, especially at the community college level, are only beginning their work to bridge the gaps between academic and vocational education, it is clearly a priority activity (Bragg, 1992).

The development of tech-prep is associated with previous efforts to establish articulated course agreements between community colleges and local high schools. The most widely cited research investigations of national articulation efforts were conducted by Bushnell (1978), Long *et al.* (1986) and McKinney *et al.* (1988). Based on the results from site visits and questionnaire surveys these researchers offered recommendations for successful articulation efforts. Bushnell (1978) found a necessity for adequate counseling services, placement services, and developmental or remedial education programs. Long *et al.* (1986) found that a true blending of resources at secondary and post-secondary institutions required creating a jointly operated training facility; writing new, comprehensive, competency-based curricula for all four years; and investing substantial planning time and funding. McKinney *et al.* (1988) found that the increasing state role in articulation can be centered most usefully on removing bureaucratic hurdles, providing information and ensuring continuity in financial support, and educating all potential stakeholders as to their potential benefits of early involvement.

Results from recent investigations (Dornsife, 1992; Hull and Parnell, 1991) substantiate previous findings. For instance, researchers continue to report that investment of substantial planning time and funding is a key factor contributing to the implementation of tech-prep initiatives (Bragg, Layton and Hammons, forthcoming; National Council for Occupational Education, 1989; Ramer, 1991; Evaluation and Training Institute, 1991; Wentling *et al.*, 1991). More importantly, results from recent investigations indicate that the few programs that have operated for at least five years have advanced their scope and objectives beyond the articulation of existing courses that merely provide advanced placement credit (Dornsife, 1992; Ramer, 1991). However, the introduction of tech-prep is leading to a broader concept of articulation — one that expands the concept from individual course articulation to the articulation of full-blown programs or majors.

A second kind of improvement may occur when consortia move, over time, from the simpler, advanced credit mode to the more complex, advanced skills mode, in which programs are designed to add specific technical content to programs and not merely shorten the time it takes to acquire the same knowledge. However, most tech-prep

Table 24: *Initial implementation of tech-prep: components completed*

Initial implementation stage (five highest mean scores)	Ranked by mean score (score range from 1–5)
consortium building (including recruiting schools, college, employers, and other organizations)	4.1
formal signed articulation agreements between secondary and post-secondary schools	4.0
joint in-service of secondary and post-secondary personnel (for example, faculty, counselors, administrators);	3.8
team building to facilitate tech-prep planning and implementation	3.8
equal access for all students	3.6

programs are in the earlier stages of development and have not as yet achieved these more advanced forms of articulation.

Tech-prep Planning and Implementation

To qualify for a tech-prep grant, local consortia — taking on a multitude of forms but typically comprised of a public community college and its surrounding secondary school districts and businesses and industries must develop a plan to address components specified in the legislation. The idea of using a consortium-type approach may enhance the potential for implementation of an educational innovation, but research suggests the act of involving multiple entities may require a significant portion of the three-year time allotted for tech-prep implementation (Layton and Bragg, 1992). Consequently, it may be difficult for tech-prep to demonstrate significant impact on constituencies (for example, educational institutions, students, businesses) due to this protracted adoption period.

Bragg, Layton, and Hammons (forthcoming) found that, of the approximately 390 local tech-prep coordinators who responded to a questionnaire, most consortia have *completed* initial implementation of the following components: 'consortium building (including recruiting schools, college, employers, and other organizations); formal signed articulation agreements between secondary and post-secondary schools; joint in-service of secondary and post-secondary personnel (for example, faculty, counselors, administrators); team building to facilitate tech-prep planning and implementation; and equal access for all students' (pp. 8–9). Scores on a scale measuring degree of implementation are shown in table 24, for the components with the highest implementation scores.

Table 25:   Components in tech-prep planning stage

Planning stage (five lowest mean scores)	Ranked by mean score (score range from 1–5)
apprenticeships spanning secondary and post-secondary education	2.0
computer monitoring of student progress through tech-prep programs	2.1
job placement services for students/graduates	2.5
work-based learning for students (for example, internships, apprenticeships)	2.6
development of advanced skills technical curriculum.	2.7

Components still in the planning stage include: apprenticeships spanning secondary and post-secondary education; computer monitoring of student progress through tech-prep programs; job placement services for students/graduates; work-based learning for students (for example, internships, apprenticeships); and development of advanced skills technical curriculum. As shown in table 25, these are the program elements with the lowest implementation ratings.

Control of tech-prep funding and administration primarily rests within traditional state and local vocational education agencies, possibly to the detriment of the initiative in the long term. Many of the tech-prep coordinators interviewed by Bragg (1992) described problems occurring with implementation when tech-prep was isolated from the entire educational enterprise and viewed as another vocational education program. This focus was viewed as particularly threatening to effectively integrating vocational and academic subject matter, an essential feature of tech-prep. Release of general education federal or state funds for tech-prep could create a fairer and more realistic environment for implementation of the integration concept called for in the Perkins II legislation.

Partnerships are a necessity for full implementation of tech-prep, according to the federal legislation. Depending upon past and current relationships, some tech-prep planners seemed to be struggling with establishing fair and meaningful partnerships among:

- the levels of education (i.e., high school and two-year college, or two-year college and four-year college),
- academic and vocational education teaching and curricula; and
- education and business, industry, and labor constituencies.

For example, sometimes business and industry or post-secondary education was viewed as trying to exert too much control over high school

Table 26:   Most important barriers to tech-prep implementation

Barrier	Ranked by mean score (score range from 1–6)
Little time designated for joint planning by academic and vocational or secondary and post-secondary faculty.	4.2
Failure of four-year colleges and universities to award college credit for applied academic or other tech-prep courses.	4.1
Lack of general awareness about tech-prep.	4.1
Lack of staff, time, and money dedicated to tech-prep.	4.0
Belief that tech-prep is an educational 'fad' that will go away.	3.8

Table 27:   Least important barriers to tech-prep implementation

Barrier	Ranked by mean score (score range from 1–5)
Lack of cooperation from teachers' unions	2.0
Pressure from special interest groups to modify the tech-prep effort	2.1
Too much flexibility in local implementation of tech-prep	2.3
Lack of support from labor organizations	2.3
Failure of two-year post-secondary schools to accommodate tech-prep students	2.3

curricula. In other cases, either vocational or academic education was seen as too aggressive in establishing the newly-articulated tech-prep curricula. In still other cases, four-year colleges were refusing to consider tech-prep curriculum as comparable to college prep. In sum, without meaningful partnerships, it will be difficult to establish tech-prep effectively. Both state and local educational agencies seemed to be learning under fire about what could influence the success and failure of their new partnerships.

According to the survey conducted by Bragg, Layton, and Hammons (forthcoming), the five most important barriers to tech-prep implementation were as follows: 'Little time designated for joint planning by academic and vocational or secondary and post-secondary faculty. Failure of four-year colleges and universities to award college credit for applied academic or other tech-prep courses. Lack of general awareness about tech-prep. Lack of staff, time, and money dedicated to tech-prep. Belief that tech-prep is an educational "fad" that will go away' (pp. 10–11). Table 26 shows the average ratings of importance given to these obstacles.

Table 27 lists the barriers that were said to be least important: 'Lack of cooperation from teachers' unions. Pressure from special interest groups to modify the tech-prep effort. Too much flexibility in local implementation of tech-prep. Lack of support from labor organizations.

Failure of two-year post-secondary schools to accommodate tech-prep students' (pp. 10–11).

Dornsife (1992) has analyzed the relationship between the components of tech-prep, the stages of program development, and the organizational structure of program operations. An overview of these relationships is presented in figure 5. This table presents a logical process through which typical tech-prep sites progress. Each part of the program — information and marketing, curriculum development, career guidance, and program evaluation — may be at a different stage of development.

Information and marketing. The purpose of information and marketing campaign is to 'spread the word', inform audiences, and promote student enrollment in articulated courses. As tech-prep programs evolve and 'take root', the purpose of these campaigns includes a focus on larger issues, such as the goals of vocational education, and the relationship between selected course offerings and technical career opportunities. Information campaigns change over time, and vary on the basis of the approach selected for planning and implementation, and the activities selected to constitute the campaign. For instance, a campaign can be carried out by administrators at the post-secondary institution, personnel in the district office, by a committee or task force, or by an outside specialist hired as a consultant. In addition, the selected marketing activities may be singular or multiple, and may take place during the entire year, or coincide with specific events during the school-year.

Curriculum development. At the heart of tech-prep programs is the development of articulated curriculum between secondary and post-secondary institutions. Although there is widespread agreement on a definition of articulation, and the processes for developing articulated curriculum, there remain several variations in actual practice. In short, while most schools follow the same steps for articulating tech-prep curriculum the result is not always the development of similar programs. Given these variations, the material below provides a discussion of some current curriculum variations.

Given the potential difficulties in planning and implementing tech-prep, most schools begin by choosing the path of least resistance and articulate similar courses currently available. At this beginning stage of development, the primary objective is to articulate curriculum that prevents duplication of coursework, and shortens the time for secondary students to complete a post-secondary program.

A second approach to curriculum articulation is to modify the content of existing courses, and to articulate a sequence of secondary

Figure 5: The evolution of tech-prep programs: development stages of program components

PROGRAM COMPONENTS

PROGRAM DEVELOPMENT STAGES	Information/marketing campaign	Course articulation and curriculum development	Career guidance	Program improvement
Beginning (in operation approx. 1–2 yrs.)	initiate small-scale 'spread-the-word' campaign	articulation of currently existing individual courses in vocational-technical program areas	establish Career Guidance Center (for example, rearrange offices, upgrade equipment)	identify outcome indicators (for example, enrollment figures) and context and process indicators (for example, student satisfaction with curriculum), establish baselines, and informally collect information
Intermediate (in operation approx. 2–3 yrs.)	establish a formal/written marketing plan, identify all target audiences, develop and implement a sequence of specific marketing activities	articulation of modified courses, and course sequences in voc-tech program areas	expand career development program at secondary level (grades 7–12)	formalize system for collecting data, review and expand indicators as needed
Advanced (in operation approx. 3–4+ yrs.)	engage in major marketing campaign, wide-spread dissemination of program description and outcomes, expand permanent program activities	articulation of completely new courses, course sequences, and the development of voc-tech and academic core curriculum, and programs that provide training along a career ladder	integrate career development programs to all school levels (grades K–14)	routinely analyze program improvement data, revise components as needed, publish results

Source: Dornsife (1992) p. 5.

courses in one or more vocational-technical program areas. In most secondary and post-secondary institutions, course modifications consist of integrating new occupation-related information and skills. This integration can take the form of using new textbooks, new and different computerized material (for example, word-processing packages), or new equipment and machinery (for example, computerized milling machines). Beyond these course changes, the most common form of curriculum modification for tech-prep programs is the adoption of competency-based approaches to coursework.

The third approach to developing tech-prep curriculum is to articulate new courses, as well as course sequences, and to develop academic and vocational-technical core curriculum designed to provide training along a career ladder. In some schools, this third approach to developing curriculum is the result of direction provided by state initiatives or legislative mandates.

In the case of tech-prep, the articulation of new courses is almost synonymous with the integration of 'applied academic courses' into a core curriculum for vocational-technical programs. These courses emphasize the acquisition of academic principles and concepts through classroom and laboratory activities that connect abstract knowledge to workplace applications.

The advantage of using applied academic courses is that they can serve as a coherent sequence of core courses linked to a sequence of recommended or required vocational courses. This linkage is a major objective of tech-prep programs, and provides the student with a clear educational plan to meet his/her occupational goals.

For example, as shown below in table 28, an articulated sequence of classes in tech-prep is offered between Portland Community College and Hillsboro Union High School (Portland, Oregon). A student interested in business administration occupations (accounting) completes a sequence of coursework that includes academic courses required for graduation, and recommended vocational (business) and academic courses to be taken during the junior and senior years (for example, accounting I, computer applications for business, and algebra I). In the process the student can earn community college credit in eight of the twelve recommended courses. In turn, if the student continues in the associate degree accounting program, he/she can earn transfer credit to a four-year college in eighteen of the twenty-seven courses required for graduation.

In this example the tech-prep curriculum is presented as a coherent sequence of *academic* courses linked with a sequence of *vocational-technical* courses. This sequencing provides students with a clear

Table 28: Hillsboro High School 2 plus 2 sequence of classes tech-prep associate degree in accounting

High school — 2		Community college — +2	
Junior year	**Senior year**	**First year**	**Second Year**
semester 1	**semester 1**	**first term**	**fourth term**
required course	*required course*	*intro/business	*mgmt fundmtls
English	English	business math	*bas cost acctg
US history	economics	intro/acctg	*princ econ
personal finance		keyboarding I	macroecon
		*English comp	general educ
recommended	*recommended*	**second term**	**fifth term**
essentials algebra	+algebra 1	*princ/acctg 1	*princ/acctg
+accounting I	accounting 2	*business law	*special studies acctg
+intro word-	+computer	*income tax	problems
processing	applic/bus	*bus mach/calc	*princ/econ: microecon
	physical science	*bus comm	elective
			general educ
semester 2	**semester 2**	**third term**	**sixth term**
required course	*required course*	*comp in bus	*analyzing fin statements
English	English	*acctg apps	*finance elective
US history	social studies	*princ/acct II	general education
health		princ/econ	
		elective	
recommended	*recommended*		
essential for alg	+algebra 1		
+acctg I	accounting 2		
+word processing	+computer appl/bus		
applic	physical science		
+ = college credit available		* = college transfer	

Source: Student Guide, Portland Community College, and Hillsboro Union High School District, Hillsboro, OR, (1990) p. 10.

educational plan, and, in many technical program areas, it provides the student with 'multiple exits', or training along a 'career ladder'. For example, the accounting course sequence at Hillsboro Union High School is designed to provide the student with entry-level skills needed for immediate employment, or for continuing in an accounting program at a post-secondary institution such as Portland Community College.

In several cases, the development of tech-prep curriculum at the advanced stage of program development is the result of collaborative efforts with business and industry representatives. Their direct input typically includes suggestions for revising existing curriculum associated with the routine upgrading of local jobs (for example, integrating widely used computer packages into the curriculum of business, administrative, and drafting courses). In some cases, however, the input from business and industry is required for the development of new courses to provide training for new or changing employment needs in the community (for example, the development of tech-prep in hazardous waste materials technology).

Career guidance. The third operational component of tech-prep programs is career guidance (Chew, 1992). The purpose of this component is to prepare a sequence of support activities designed to help students plan and develop career options. Guidance activities serve a supportive role for education initiatives such as tech-prep because the sequencing of career development activities helps students gain an understanding of the relationship between school and work. In general, the guidance activities for tech-prep are designed to promote student development at both the secondary and post-secondary level. In most schools, the implementation of these activities requires a redefinition of guidance at the secondary level. Instead of an ancillary department or a series of fragmented and event-oriented activities (for example, a self-esteem workshop or a career day), the guidance program is restructured into an organized sequence of activities designed to help students learn how to plan and develop their career.

The actual selection of guidance activities is unique to each school. However, at the early stage of tech-prep development there are few detailed examples of developing or developed guidance programs coordinated with tech-prep. For instance, in most schools a centrally located guidance center provides students with a collection of up-to-date print and non-print career information. This information is disseminated through various activities for improving grade-level career awareness and exploration. Some secondary school districts are expanding their sequence of guidance activities to include students in grades 7 and 8, such as requiring that all eighth grade students complete a 'career plan' form. The information on this form indicates what course of study and corresponding classes (for example, college prep, tech-prep) the student has selected, it is included in his/her career planning folder, and it must be signed by the parents and the student. The State of Florida is perhaps an exemplar in these efforts with the enactment in 1991 of 'Blueprint 2000: A System of School Improvement and Accountability'. This legislation included 'Blueprint for Career Preparation' which has resulted in 64 per cent of all eight graders completing career plans during 1991/92 (United States General Accounting Office (GAO), 1993).[2]

In general, the lack of comprehensive guidance programs is not the result of disagreement over the importance of guidance for tech-prep, but, instead, the result of limited funding. The development of a comprehensive guidance program, one that, for instance, includes work-site internships for teachers and students, requires financial resources and staff commitments that many schools do not have. As a result of these limitations, the necessary guidance activities tend to develop at a slightly slower pace than the other operational components.

Program evaluation. The fourth operational component of tech-prep initiatives is program evaluation. It too is a dynamic process. Given the nature of the evaluation process, and because *most* programs have only been operational for one to three years, there is a limited amount of published material describing current evaluation efforts. In fact, most administrators believe it takes five to seven years of operation before a comprehensive evaluation can be conducted and any major program improvements instituted (Hull, 1987; Ohio State University, 1990). Furthermore, during the first year of operation most administrators collect information for evaluation purposes through informal means (for example, telephone calls, unscheduled meetings, etc.). In turn, there is a limited amount of published data, and restricted access to any information contained in school records (an exception is the study by Hammons, 1992).

In most cases, the community college assumes primary responsibility for conducting a program evaluation, publishing the results, and initiating program improvements. Secondary school personnel participate in these efforts; however, their participation is often limited by the form and content of data they can provide. For instance, most secondary schools do not have the financial or personnel resources to maintain a complete academic and career development profile on all students in tech-prep programs, or to collect feedback from community members after they attend school events, such as parent's night or an open house. Despite these limitations, a thorough evaluation of tech-prep programs includes the participation of all 'stakeholders' (for example, counselors, students, employers), particularly the collaborating secondary and post-secondary institutions.

It is important to note that a national evaluation of tech-prep is being conducted for the Office of Vocational and Adult Education (OVAE) by Mathematica (Princeton, New Jersey). The five-year evaluation plan includes a questionnaire survey and site visits.

Notes

1   Hayward refers to other researchers in the description of these analytic approaches. For 'reliability-corrected covariance analysis' see Lord (1960) and Porter (1967). For 'gap-reduction evaluation design', see Tallmadge, Lam and Gamel (1987).

2   This Career Preparation Plan is developed after a student has participated in 'self- and career-awareness programs in grades K-5, personal assessment and technological literacy in grade 6, and career orientation and exploration in grades 7 and 8. In grades 9 through 12, students are expected to engage in academic and specialized skill development, while in postsecondary education they are expected to pursue skill development and career advancement' (GAO, 1993, pg. 22).

5   Programs for Out-of-School Youth

Numerous programs have attempted to improve the job prospects of young people who are not in school and are looking for work. Evaluations of these efforts have concluded that the resources and structures of these programs are largely unable to overcome problems related to family structure, neighborhood structure, education, and health (US Department of Labor, Employment and Training Administration, 1992). Furthermore, the developmental stage of youth in these programs is not fully taken into account in the present employment and training system (Gambone, 1993).

The results of studies that have used either a strong quasi-experimental design or a random-assignment experiment are shown in table 29. These measure the earning-enhancing effects of programs for out-of-school youth — young people who have not completed high school, and whose employment prospects are therefore poorest. Other studies and programs have been described in Taggart (1981), Hahn and Lerman (1985) and Betsey, Hollister and Papageorgiou (1985).

A random-assignment evaluation has been conducted of participants in JTPA programs. Early results of that evaluation have been reported by Bloom, Orr, Cave, Bell and Doolittle (1992). Table 29 contains some of those results. They indicate negative or null effects for youth.

The program with the best record for improving the earnings of disadvantaged, out-of-school youth is the Job Corps. Originally authorized by the Economic Opportunity Act of 1964, it was incorporated into CETA in 1973, then JTPA in 1982, and has since been expanded further. Table 29 shows some of the results from an evaluation by Mathematica, Inc., as summarized in Betsey, Hollister and Papageorgiou (1985). Although participants were not randomly assigned to the program and comparison group, the comparison group was matched on various characteristics and was taken from geographic areas where participation in Job Corps was low. Gains in earnings for Job Corps participants were more than $600 in the second year after they finished or left the

Table 29: Point estimates of increment in annual earnings resulting from programs for out-of-school youth

Betsey, Hollister, and Papageorgiou (1985)-Review of evidence on youth employment and training programs.

Job Corps residential training for disadvantaged youth (Mathematica Inc. evaluation by Mallar et al. used non-randomly assigned matched comparison group). Effects on weekly earnings x 50, in 1977 dollars:

Second year after program termination	$627
Third year after program termination	545
Fourth year after program termination	390

Ventures in Community Improvement (VICI) temporary employment in construction work for disadvantaged youth (evaluation by Corp. for Public/Private Ventures used non-randomly assigned comparison group).

Effect on annual earnings in 1980: $1288

Bloom, Orr, Cave, Bell, and Doolittle (1992)-Random-assignment evaluation of JTPA.

Sum of earnings in third through sixth quarters after assignment to program (assignment occurred 11/87 through 9/89). Average difference between assignees and control group, age 16–21:

	Classroom training	On-the-job training/job search	Other
Men	–54	–1036	–900
Women	–143	57	–134

Cave and Doolittle (1991)-Random-assignment evaluation.

Jobstart non-residential training program for disadvantaged out-of-school youth. Effect on earnings in 1987/88, two years after assignment.

Men	$–667
Women living with own child(ren)	172
Women not living with own child(ren)	202

Manpower Demonstration Research Corporation (1980)-Random-assignment evaluation of National Supported Work Demonstration.

Effects on annual earnings of young dropouts 1977 to 3/79, 13–24 months after enrollment in sample:	$131

program, and remained just under $400 two years after that. These amounts are in 1977 dollars; in early-1990s dollars they would be worth about twice as much. Another late-1970s program for out-of-school youth, also described by Betsey *et al.* and summarized in table 29, produced a gain of $1288, but the quasi-experimental evaluation was not as rigorous as the evaluation of Job Corps.

A less expensive, non-residential version of Job Corps training, called Jobstart, was conducted in the late 1980s and evaluated using random assignment. Table 29 gives interim results as reported by Cave and Doolittle (1991). In the second year after assignment, young men in the program earned $667 *less* than the control group. Effects for women were positive but small. Since some of the participants were still in training during the second year, effects may be more positive in the fourth year, when the evaluation is scheduled to end.

An earlier program, the Supported Work Demonstration of the late 1970s, also was evaluated using random assignment, and also failed to find any substantial positive effect for young high school dropouts. Some results are shown in table 29, from Manpower Demonstration Research Corporation (1980). So far, there does not appear to have been any federally supported program for out-of-school youth that has been found by random-assignment evaluation to produce significant gains in earnings.

These findings have generated multiple recommendations for improved programs for youth. Gambone (1993) proposes system-wide attention to specific components of youth education and training programs. These features are:

- comprehensive assessments;
- regular monitoring of the developmental status and needs of youth as they move through programs;
- high-quality work experience and educational components that engage youth, and hold them in programs for a period sufficient to allow them to derive developmental benefits;
- opportunities to participate in teams, discuss important life issues, and participate in the governance of programs;
- one-to-one relationships with adults trained in understanding and facilitating the developmental process;
- support services aimed at those problems that typically prevent disadvantaged youth from maintaining their participation in program interventions, such as lack of shelter;
- program structures and activities that promote and implement principles of fairness; and
- organizations that operate with a clear mission, leadership culture and climate oriented toward providing a supportive environment for youth. (p. 68)

In some instances, JTPA programs have coordinated with other service providers in local areas to improve programs and limit redundancies. Grubb *et al.* (1990) have presented models of JTPA coordination with vocational education that have been exemplary in the field. For instance, JTPA has subcontracts with providers in vocational schools and community colleges. Programs, STEP and others, are offered jointly by service providers who share administrative and funding responsibilities. Further, JTPA funds have been used to provide ancillary services, like child care and counseling, for these programs. Regional boards have also developed to make joint decisions about program offerings and funding decisions in service delivery areas. These kinds of efforts are consistent with the recommendations to improve the planning, coordination and follow-up of programs.

6   Strategic Choices

Encouraged by federal legislation, states and localities are building new school-to-work systems. The purpose is to prepare young people more effectively for their immediate or eventual careers, by creating more coherent and visible pathways from high school to work. Along these pathways, young people are to be given more and better opportunities for learning in the workplace itself.

This report has reviewed the US research pertaining to these efforts. Because fully fledged school-to-work systems do not yet exist in this country, the research has dealt with separate school-to-work programs and program models. These programs and models are of two kinds: school-*and*-work arrangements which permit students to participate in both kinds of activity during the same time period, and school-*for*-work programs which provide instruction with the express purpose of preparing students for work. Cooperative education and new youth apprenticeships are major examples of school-and-work programs. School-for-work programs include secondary and post-secondary vocational education — both traditional versions and newer models such as tech-prep and career academies.

What can state and local decision-makers learn from the research that may inform the strategic decisions they face in designing new school-to-work systems? Probably the most fundamental decision is whether the new system will be designed only for the 'non-college-bound', or whether it will be more inclusive (see Bailey and Merritt, 1993; Rosenbaum, 1992). This choice has a direct bearing on what kind of school-based instruction, and what kind of work-based learning, should be offered. In this chapter, we discuss these choices in the light of findings from the research.

The issue of which students to include in school-to-work programs is linked to the historical debate about vocational education in this country. Since 1917, federally funded vocational education has prepared students only for 'occupations requiring other than a baccalaureate or advanced degree'. The evidence reviewed in this report confirms that high school vocational students are, in fact, less likely to go to college. Compared to other high school students who also do not attend college, vocational students on average earn higher wages — but only if they find jobs related to their training, which most do not. Similar results have been found for students who participate in cooperative education (co-op). At the high school level co-op has mainly been part of vocational education. There is ample evidence that co-op succeeds in linking work-based and school-based learning in students' minds. However, the evidence does not indicate that co-op generally leads to higher earnings after high school, unless students continue working with their co-op employer. Co-op students' economic prospects are also diminished by the fact that they are less likely to attend college compared to other high school graduates.

In recent years the financial return to a four-year college degree reached an all-time high. Four-year college graduates earn substantially larger salaries than graduates of two-year colleges, who earn more than those with no post-secondary education. Limiting new school-to-work systems only to non-college-bound students thus limits the possible future earnings of participants in the new systems. In effect, such a decision would reproduce in the new system one of the defining characteristics of traditional vocational education.

Beyond the direct negative effect on students' possible future earnings, excluding college-bound students would also detract from the image of the new school-to-work system itself. Because a four-year college degree is now, more than ever, a ticket to the highest-paying jobs, the more ambitious students in high school tend to choose college-prep programs. In 1992 the proportion of high school graduates aiming for a four-year college degree reached an all-time high. A parent explained, 'we've got two very clear tracks right now — college prep and "nowhere" prep' (Jobs for the Future, 1993b, p. 11) If new school-to-work pathways are identified with the non-college-bound, or with the non-baccalaureate-bound, it will be difficult for them to avoid being identified as 'nowhere prep'. Research on implementation of the tech-prep model has already found that a major barrier is the failure of four-year colleges and universities to award credit for tech-prep courses in two-year colleges (table 26, above).

Even in Germany, whose 'dual system' is often considered a model to be emulated by new school-to-work structures in the US, the growing demand for higher education is requiring the system to provide easier access from apprenticeship to university. In the early 1990s the number of students in higher education for the first time surpassed the number of apprentices in Germany. Steedman (1993) observes, 'A relatively new phenomenon is now being noted, namely, the difficulty being experienced even by the most prestigious engineering firms in recruiting trainees of the necessary high ability and aptitude. Respected commentators . . . have, as a result, diagnosed a crisis of the whole training system arguing that if the high-cost high-quality training provision of the prestigious industrial companies is discontinued in favor of recruitment from higher education, then the credibility of the system as a whole will be undermined' (p. 1288). To prevent students' demand for university education from undermining the dual system, 'The social partners (business and labor) share the view that the transition to higher education institutions and universities should also be ensured or at least made easier for graduates of the dual system' according to a senior official in the agency that oversees that system (Laur-Ernst, 1992. p. 40).

School-to-work programs and systems can be designed so that the four-year college option is clearly left open. Some career academies have demonstrated that this is possible, even when they have taken a large proportion of students who are identified in ninth grade as being at risk of not completing high school. Career academies and some career magnet schools illustrate that high school students who are not clearly college-bound can be well served by programs that do not limit their enrollment to this 'forgotten half' only.

There are also practical reasons for students who do go to college to participate in a school-to-work program while in high school: While working their way through college, as most students now do, those who have had some practical vocational and work-based instruction while in high school may be able to earn higher hourly pay, and therefore potentially have more time available for study. Later on, their early practical training may also make them more effective in their eventual professions.

Keeping the option open does not mean that all or most students will actually go to a four-year college or university. School-to-work systems certainly must include large numbers of students who do not enroll in a baccalaureate program as soon as they finish high school. But keeping the option open avoids trying to sort students ahead of time, limiting students' future career prospects, and stigmatizing the new school-to-work system.

The main disadvantage of trying to keep the baccalaureate option open is that teachers may find it more difficult to accommodate a heterogeneous group of students, especially if they have not done so in the past. In addition, employers may balk at the idea of offering training slots to students who subsequently do not come to work in the industry. These are some of the concerns that state and local authorities will encounter as they decide how inclusive to make the new school-to-work systems.

Within the schools, major decisions must be made about the curriculum of school-to-work programs. New career majors or career pathways could consist of a set of existing courses that students may elect to follow in some logical sequence. Or they could be whole new schools-within-schools, with groups of students and teachers who stay together for a year or more, and curricula that build interdisciplinary linkages around particular career themes such as computers or health occupations. Career academies, tech-prep, new youth apprenticeship and career magnet programs have developed integrated, interdisciplinary curricula of this kind. The 1990 amendments to the Carl Perkins Act required that federal funds for vocational education now be spent only on programs that integrate academic and vocational education, and the 1994 School to Work Opportunities Act provides additional incentives. However, high schools, and even two-year colleges, are not mainly concerned with vocational education or school-to-work programs. Building integrated curricula for large numbers of students will require the active collaboration of non-vocational teachers and departments. Administrators and counselors will have to help with scheduling, guidance, and all the myriad details involved in launching a new effort. The strategic question for high schools and two-year colleges is whether to make this kind of commitment, or simply take the easy way out.

Keeping the four-year college option open adds to the challenge of building an integrated curriculum. Four-year colleges and universities require applicants to take certain prerequisite courses, earn good grades, and perform well on admission tests. In order for students to meet these requirements, new school-to-work programs must cover the necessary bases. Again, career academies and career magnet schools have shown that it is possible to provide a career-related curriculum that prepares students either for full-time work or for four-year college, but these are not simple programs.

In addition to school-based instruction, school-to-work systems are to give new emphasis to work-based learning. The main strategic question here is whether work-based learning will be designed primarily to prepare students for immediate employment, or to develop general cognitive abilities. These are not contradictory purposes, but they do have different implications for the use of students' time. Preparation for immediate employment implies learning the specific skills and routines necessary to do a particular job for a particular employer. Cooperative education in high schools has had some success in accomplishing this purpose. But there is evidence that co-op results in higher earnings for students only if they stay with their co-op employer. There seems to be a problem with the portability of skills and knowledge from one employer to another. Development of new skill standards for occupations and industries — an important component of new school-to-work systems — may solve that problem.

However, there is still a question of whether students' time in workplaces should be spent mainly learning how to do the work, or whether students should also be using the workplace as a setting to learn other things (Miller, Watts, and Jamieson, 1991). They can be given independent learning assignments related to their academic courses: for instance, how math is used in quality control. More generally, they can be given problem-solving assignments, individually or in groups, that require them to use what they know from various academic courses, to obtain other relevant information, and to bring it all to bear on a practical matter. This kind of exercise can help develop students' thinking abilities, and can also be useful to employers.

The question of emphasis on learning to do the work versus learning to think is related to the issue of students' probable futures. Programs only for the non-college-bound will presumably emphasize preparation for immediate employment. If they are geared to 'high-performance workplaces', they will also emphasize the development of thinking. Programs that keep open the four-year college option will aim to prepare students for immediate employment and develop their thinking abilities, but will also put more emphasis on the application of academic learning.

Although the research reviewed in this report is fairly voluminous, the questions are complex, and there are few definitive answers. Even when programs have been found to be effective, it is usually not possible to say exactly why they are effective, because the programs themselves are multi-faceted. Furthermore, each program model — youth apprenticeship, tech-prep, co-op, career academy, or community college vocational education, for example — has been implemented differently in different places. This will continue to be true unless program standards are enacted and enforced, which seems unlikely. But program standards may not be necessary or desirable, if academic and occupational skill standards are put in place, as called for by the Goals 2000: Educate America Act of 1994. Implementation of skill standards will involve measuring what students know and can do, both in school and at work. Students' performance is what matters most. If new school-to-work programs can improve students' performance, public authorities need not worry about whether certain program components are included.

Finally, it is useful to recall again that school-to-work transition seldom means an abrupt transition from full-time schooling to full-time employment. The initial transition from school to work usually occurs over a period of several years, during which work is combined with school. A successful school-to-work transition system will use this initial transition period to help young people find and keep the kind of full-time job they want, with a minimum of wasted time. But it will also do more than that. A successful system will enable young people to master the process of learning while they work. In a fast-changing economy, this is fundamental.

Appendix A: Examples of School-To-Work Programs, and Program Elements

Program type	Industry	Project start date	Primary source of funding	Grade levels
Apprenticeship				
Broome YADP	tech/health	1991	foundation/emp	11–14
Craftsmanship 2000	metalworking	1992	local partnership	11–14
Maine YAP	variety	1992	colleges/emp	11–13
NATPC	food	1977	self (ACF)	13–15
Penn YAP	metalworking	1991	D of L/JFF	11–14
Pickens County YAI	electronics	1992	JFF/emp	11–14
Project ProTech	health	1991	US D of L	11–14
West Virginia YAP	variety		CCSSO/D of L	9–12
Wisconsin YAP	(four)	1991	state/employer	11+
Co-op				
CWEE	technology	1972	school dist.	11–12
EIF	electronics	1979	DofL/industry	9–12
Partnership Project	retail/manufacturing	1984	foundation/ind	11–12
Quality Conn.	banking	1990	industry/NAB	9+
School-to-apprenticeship				
CAVC	variety	1980	sc. dist./emp	11–12
Great Oaks JVSD	variety		school/emp	12
Project Mechtech	manufacturing	1990	US D of L	11–12
Academies				
ALIVE	tech/finance	1990	wide variety	10–12
BFA	finance	1984		
FSTA	finance	1984		10–12
Workforce LA	finance/tech.	1989	DofL/industry	K–12
Work readiness				
Step Ahead		1985		
Dropout prevention				
Cambridge-Lesley	education	1991	school/college	11–12
COFFEE	variety	1979	sc. dist/ind	any
MD's Tomorrow		1990	US D of L	9–12

Miscellaneous

Career prep	metals/finance	(in dev.)	state/emp	11-adult
Education for Employment	variety		state/employer	
Job Readiness		1984		
PPPP		1980		9–12
RR 2000	(six)	1992	school/JFF	9–12
SWAP		1984		10–12

Program	Pre-11th preparation: Academic	Career exploration	Selection criteria	Parent involvement	Curriculum: Academic and vocational	Builds on work experience
Apprenticeship						
Broome YADP			broad		yes	yes
Craftsmanship 2000			broad		yes	
Maine YAP		yes	broad			
NATPC			broad			
Penn YAP			non-college	yes	yes	yes
Pickens County YAI		yes	non-college	yes	yes	yes
Project ProTech			at-risk		yes	yes
West Virginia YAP		yes	broad		yes	
Wisconsin YAP		yes	non-college		yes	
Co-op						
CWEE			non-college			
EIF			non-college		yes	yes
Partnership Project			at-risk	yes		
Quality Conn.	yes	yes	at-risk		yes	yes
School-to-apprenticeship						
CAVC			non-college			
Great Oaks JVSD			broad			
Project Mechtech			broad		yes	
Academies						
ALIVE	yes	yes	broad		yes	yes
BFA			at-risk		yes	
FSTA		yes	at-risk	yes	yes	
Workforce LA	yes	yes	broad	yes	yes	
Work readiness						
Step Ahead			broad		yes	
Dropout prevention						
Cambridge-Lesley			at-risk		yes	yes
COFFEE			at-risk		yes	yes
MD's Tomorrow	yes	yes	at-risk	yes		
Miscellaneous						
Career prep			broad		yes	yes
Education for Employment					yes	
Job Readiness			at-risk	yes	yes	
PPPP			above ave.	yes	yes	
RR 2000	yes	yes	at-risk		yes	yes
SWAP			at-risk			

Program	Counseling	Work experience: When?	Paid?	Training plan?	Who finds placement?	Who supervises?
Apprenticeship						
Broome YADP	yes	all-year	yes	yes	student (@ firms)	school
Craftsmanship 2000		all-year	yes			
Maine YAP						
NATPC		all-year	yes	yes		app. com
Penn YAP		all-year	yes	yes	program	school/ employer
Pickens County YAI		all-year	yes		program	
Project ProTech		school year	yes	yes	program	
West Virginia YAP	yes	all-year	yes	yes	student (w/help)	
Wisconsin YAP		all-year	yes	yes	student (w/help)	school
Co-op						
CWEE	yes	all-year	yes	yes	program	
EIF		all-year	no			
Partnership Project	yes	all-year	yes		program	
Quality Conn.		all-year	yes	yes	student (@ firms)	employer
School-to-apprenticeship						
CAVC	yes	all-year	yes	yes	student (@ firms)	employer
Great Oaks JVSD		all-year			program	
Project Mechtech	yes	summer	yes		program	
Academies						
ALIVE		depends on acad.	some		program	
BFA		summer	yes		student (w/help)	
FSTA		summer	yes			
Workforce LA	yes					
Work readiness						
Step Ahead	yes					
Dropout prevention						
Cambridge-Lesley	yes	school year				employer
COFFEE	yes					
MD's Tomorrow	yes	short term			program	
Miscellaneous						
Career Prep						
Education for Employment	yes	all-year	yes		student	
Job Readiness	yes	summer	yes			
PPPP		all-year			program	
RR 2000		school year				school
SWAP					student	

Program	Staff development	Employer involvement: design curriculum	Materials and equipment	Speakers/ field trips	Teacher internships	Mentor
Apprenticeship						
Broome YADP		yes				yes
Craftsmanship 2000	yes	yes				yes
Maine YAP						
NATPC						
Penn YAP	yes	yes				yes
Pickens County YAI	yes	yes		yes		yes
Project ProTech						yes
West Virginia YAP						
Wisconsin YAP		yes				yes
Co-op						
CWEE						
EIF		yes	yes	yes	yes	
Partnership Project				yes		yes
Quality Conn.		yes				yes
School-to-apprenticeship						
CAVC						
Great Oaks JVSD						
Project Mechtech						yes
Academies						
ALIVE	yes	yes	yes	yes	yes	yes
BFA				yes		yes
FSTA			yes	yes		
Workforce LA	yes	yes		yes		yes
Work readiness						
Step Ahead			yes	yes		
Dropout prevention						
Cambridge-Lesley				yes		yes
COFFEE			yes	yes	yes	
MD's Tomorrow	yes	yes				yes
Miscellaneous						
Career Prep						yes
Education for Employment						
Job Readiness		yes	yes	yes	yes	
PPPP	yes	yes	yes	yes	yes	
RR 2000	yes			yes		
SWAP	yes			yes		yes

Program	Post-secondary linkage	Expected outcomes	Performance standards	Formal evaluation?
Apprenticeship				
Broome YADP				
Craftsmanship 2000	4	occ. cert.		
Maine YAP	4	o/c; post-sec.		
NATPC	articulation	occ. cert.		
Penn YAP	articulation	occ. cert.	competencies	
Pickens County YAI	2+2	occ. cert.		
Project ProTech	4	post-sec. ed.		
West Virginia YAP	art./2+2	o/c; post-sec.	attendance	
Wisconsin YAP		o/c; post-sec.		
Co-op				
CWEE				
EIF				
Partnership Project			grades	yes
Quality Conn.			att./grades	
School-to-apprenticeship				
CAVC		occ. cert.		
Great Oaks JVSD			att./grades	
Project Mechtech	4	occ. cert.		
Academies				
ALIVE	art./2+2	o/c; post-sec.	att./grades	
BFA				yes
FSTA				yes
Workforce LA	2+2/artic.		attendance	yes
Work readiness				
Step Ahead		work	yes	
Dropout prevention				
Cambridge-Lesley	articulation	post-sec. ed.		
COFFEE			att./grades	
' MD's Tomorrow				
Miscellaneous				
Career Prep	4	o/c; post-sec.	competencies	
Education for Employment	art./2+2	occ. cert.		
Job Readiness		post-sec. ed.		yes
PPPP		post-sec. ed.		yes
RR 2000		o/c; post-sec.		yes
SWAP				

Appendix B: Names and Locations of School-To-Work Programs in Appendix A

ALIVE
Academic Learning Integrating Vocational Education, Pasadena Unified School District and Jobs for the Future, Pasadena, California

BFA
Business and Finance Academy, Pittsburgh, Pennsylvania

Broome YADP
Broome County Youth Apprenticeship Demonstration Project, Cornell University College of Human Ecology, Ithaca, New York

Cambridge-Lesley
Cambridge-Lesley Careers in Education Program, Lesley College/Cambridge Rindge School of Technical Arts, Cambridge, Massachusetts

CAVC
Calhoun Area Vocational Center, Battle Creek, Michigan

Career Prep.
The Productive Chicago Career Preparation Initiative, Chicago Public Schools and City Colleges of Chicago, Chicago, Illinois,

COFFEE
Project COFFEE, Cooperative Federation For Educational Experiences, Oxford, Massachusetts

Craftsmanship 2000
Craftsmanship 2000, Inc., Tulsa, Oklahoma

CWEE
Cooperative Work Experience Education, Pittsburgh Secondary Schools, Pittsburgh, Pennsylvania

Education for Employment
Education for Employment (EFE), Kalamazoo Valley Consortium, Comstock Public Schools, Comstock, Michigan

EIF
Electronic Industries Foundation, Washington, DC

FSTA
Financial Services Technology Program, Washington, DC

Great Oaks JVSD
Great Oaks Joint Vocational School District School-to-Apprenticeship Program, Cincinnati, Ohio

Job Readiness
Job Readiness Program, Chicago, Illinois

Maine YAP
Maine Youth Apprenticeship Program, Southern Maine Technical College, South Portland, Maine

MD's Tomorrow
Maryland's Tomorrow Department of Economic and Employment Development, Carroll County, Maryland

NATPC
National Apprenticeship Training Program for Cooks, Educational Institute of the American Culinary Federation, St. Augustine, Florida

Partnership Proj.
Partnership Project, Portland School District, the Private Industry Council, and the Business Youth Exchange, Portland, Oregon

Penn. YAP
Pennsylvania Youth Apprenticeship Program, Commonwealth of Pennsylvania

Pickens Cty. YAI
Pickens County Youth Apprenticeship Initiative, Pickens County School District, Easley, South Carolina/Jobs for the Future

PPPP
Public-Private Partnership Program, Washington, DC

Project Mechtech
Maryland Mechtech, Inc./Catonsville Community College, Baltimore, Maryland

Project ProTech
Boston Private Industry Council, Boston, Massachusetts

Quality Conn.
The Quality Connection Consortium, National Alliance of Business; BankAmerica and Mission High School, San Francisco, California; Sears, Roebuck Co. and the DuPage County Illinois Area Occupational Education System

RR 2000
Roosevelt Renaissance 2000, Roosevelt High School in Portland, Oregon

Step Ahead
Step Ahead Program, Oakland High Schools, Oakland, California

SWAP
School to Work Action Program, Denver, Colorado

West Virginia YAP
West Virginia Youth Apprenticeship Program, West Virginia State Department of Education and the Council of Chief State School Officers

Wisconsin YAP
Wisconsin Youth Apprenticeship Program, Department of Industry, Labor and Human Relations; Department of Public Instruction; Wisconsin Board of Vocational, Technical and Adult Education, Madison, Wisconsin

Workforce L.A.
Los Angeles Unified School District, Los Angeles, California

References

ADLER, P.S. (Ed) (1992) *Technology and the Future of Work*, New York: Oxford University Press.

AGENCY FOR INSTRUCTIONAL TECHNOLOGY (1986a) *Implementation of Principles of Technology: Three Case Studies.*

AGENCY FOR INSTRUCTIONAL TECHNOLOGY (1986b) *Principles of Technology: Issues Related to Student Outcomes*, August.

AGENCY FOR INSTRUCTIONAL TECHNOLOGY AND CENTER FOR OCCUPATIONAL RESEARCH AND DEVELOPMENT (1984) *Principles of Technology: Unit 1: Force — Pilot Test Findings*, December.

AGENCY FOR INSTRUCTIONAL TECHNOLOGY AND CENTER FOR OCCUPATIONAL RESEARCH AND DEVELOPMENT (1985) *Principles of Technology: Unit 6: Power — Pilot Test Findings*, August.

AGENCY FOR INSTRUCTIONAL TECHNOLOGY AND CENTER FOR OCCUPATIONAL RESEARCH AND DEVELOPMENT (1986) *Principles of Technology: Unit 10: Energy Converters — Pilot Test Findings*, April.

ALTONJI, J.G. (1992) *The Effects of High School Curriculum on Education and Labor Market Outcomes*, Evanston, IL: Center for Urban Affairs and Department of Economics, Northwestern University.

AMERICAN ASSOCIATION OF COMMUNITY AND JUNIOR COLLEGES (1991) *Community College Involvement in Contracted Training and Other Economic Development Activities. A Report of a National Survey*, Washington, DC: American Association of Community and Junior Colleges, (ERIC Document No. ED 332 742).

ANGRIST, J.D. and KRUEGER, A.B. (1992) *Estimating the Payoff to Schooling Using the Vietnam-Era Draft Lottery. Working Paper No. 4067*, Cambridge, MA: National Bureau of Economic Research.

ASTIN, A.W. (1975) *Preventing Students from Dropping Out*, San Francisco, CA: Jossey-Bass.

ATTEWELL, P. (1992) 'Skill and occupational changes in US manufacturing', in ADLER, P. (Ed) *Technology and the Future of Work*, New York: Oxford University Press.

AUGENBLICK, VAN DE WATER AND ASSOCIATES (1987) *Working While Studying: Does It Matter? An Examination of the Washington Work Study Progam*, Denver, CO: AVA Education Policy/Planning Services.

BAILEY, T. (1990) *Changes in the Nature and Structure of Work: Implications for Skill Requirements and Skill Formation*, Berkeley, CA: National Center for Research in Vocational Education, University of California.

BAILEY, T. (1993) 'Can youth apprenticeship thrive in the United States?', *Educational Researcher*, 22, pp. 4–10.

BAILEY, T. and MERRITT, D. (1993) *The School-to-Work Transition and Youth Apprenticeship: Lessons from the US Experience*, New York: Manpower Demonstration Research Corporation.

BAKER, K.N. (1990) 'Rural school-based enterprise: Promise and practice in the southeast', paper presented at the annual conference of the National Rural Education Association, 1988.

BARTON, P.E. (1989) *Earning and Learning. The Academic Achievement of High-School Juniors with Jobs. The Nations's Report Card. Report No. 17-WL-01*, Princeton, NJ: National Assessment of Educational Progress, (ERIC Document No. ED 309 179).

BARTON, P.E. (1990) *From School to Work. Policy Information Report*, Princeton, NJ: Educational Testing Service, Policy Information Center, (ERIC Document No. ED 320 947).

BELLA, S.K. and HUBA, M.E. (1982) 'Student part-time jobs: The relationship between type of job and academic performance', *Journal of Student Financial Aid*, 12, pp. 22–7.

BERLIN, G. and SUM, A. (1988) *Toward More Perfect Union: Basic Skills, Poor Families, and Our Economic Future*, New York: Ford Foundation.

BERRYMAN, S.E. (1992) 'Apprenticeship as a paradigm for learning', in ROSENBAUM, J. (Ed) *Youth Apprenticeship in America: Guidelines for Building an Effective System*, Washington, DC: William T. Grant Foundation Commission on Work, Family and Citizenship.

BERRYMAN, S.E. and BAILEY, T. (1992) *The Double Helix: Education and the Economy*, New York: Teachers College Press.

BETSEY, C.L., HOLLISTER, R.G. and PAPAGEORGIOU, M.R. (Eds) (1985) *Youth Employment and Training Programs: The YEDPA Years*, Washington, DC: National Academy Press.

BISHOP, J. (1988) *Vocational Education for At-Risk Youth: How Can It Be Made More Effective? In School to Work Transition Services for Disadvantaged Youth*, Ithaca, NY: Center for Advanced Human Resources Studies, Cornell University.

BISHOP, J. (1989) 'Occupational training in high school: When does it pay off?', *Economics of Education Review*, 8, 1, pp. 1–15.

BISHOP, J. (1994) *The Payoff to Schooling and Learning in the United States*, Ithaca, NY: Cornell University, School of Industrial and Labor Relations.

BISHOP, J., BLAKEMORE, A. and LOW, S. (1985) *High School Graduates in the Labor Market: A Comparison of the Class of 1972 and 1980*, Columbus, OH: National Center for Research in Vocational Education, Ohio State University.

BISHOP, J. and CARTER. (1991) 'The worsening shortage of college-graduate workers', *Educational Evaluation and Policy Analysis*, Fall.

BLOOM, H.S., ORR, L.L., CAVE, G., BELL, S.H. and DOOLITTLE, F. (1992) *The National JTPA Study: Title II-A Impacts on Earnings and Employment at 18 Months, Executive Summary*, Bethesda, MD: Abt Associates.

BODILLY, S., RAMSEY, K., STASZ, C. and EDEN, R. (1992) *Integrating Academic and Vocational Education: Lessons from Eight Early Innovators*, Berkeley, CA: The National Center for Research in Vocational Education, University of California.

BOWERS, N. and SWAIM, P. (1992) 'Probing (some of) the issues of employment-related training and wages: Evidence from the CPS', paper presented at the Western Economic Association meetings, San Francisco, July.

BRAGG, D. (1992) 'Planning and implementation by local consortium' in BRAGG, D. (Ed) *Implementing Tech Prep: A Guide to Planning a Quality Initiative*, Berkeley, CA: National Center for Research in Vocational Education, University of California.

BRAGG, D., LAYTON, J. and HAMMONS, F. (forthcoming) *Local Tech Prep Implementation: Findings from a National Survey*, Berkeley, CA: National Center for Research in Vocational Education, University of California.

BRANTON, G.R., GYN, G. VAN., CUTT, J., LOKEN, M., NEY, T. and RICKS, F. (1990) 'A model for assessing the learning benefits in cooperative education', *Journal of Cooperative Education*, 26, 3, pp. 30–40.

BROWN, S.J. (1987) 'The impact of cooperative education on employers and graduates' in RYDER, K.G. and WILSON, J.W. (Eds) *Cooperative Education in a New Era: Understanding and Strengthening the Links Between College and the Workplace*, San Francisco, CA: Jossey-Bass. pp. 285–303.

BURGESS, E.F. (1987) 'The marketplace: Where the students run the store', *Vocational Education Journal*, August, pp. 32–3.

BURTLESS, G. (Ed) 1990 *A Future of Lousy Jobs?* Washington, DC: The Brookings Institution.

BURTLESS, G. and ORR, L. (1986) 'Are classical experiments needed for manpower policy?', *Journal of Human Resources*, 21, 4, pp. 606–39.

BUSHNELL, D. (1978) *Cooperation in Vocational Education*, Washington, DC: American Association of Community and Junior Colleges and the American Vocational Association, (ERIC Document No. ED 164 052).

CAGAMPANG, H. (1993) *Learning From School Based Work Experience Programs, Codebook: Merged Data Files for High School and Two Year College Students*, Berkeley, CA: The National Center For Research in Vocational Education, University of California.

CAHALAN, M. and FARRIS, E. (1990) *College Sponsored Tutoring and Mentoring Programs for Disadvantaged Elementary and Secondary Students. Higher Education Survey Report, Survey No. 12*, Rockville, MD: Westat, Inc, (ERIC Document No. ED 323 884).

CALIFORNIA INSTITUTE ON HUMAN SERVICES (1990) *Promising Practices for Special Needs Youth in Career-Vocational Education. Impact Programs*, Rohnert Park, CA: California Institute on Human Services, Sonoma State University, (ERIC Document No. ED 333 184).

CALIFORNIA NEW YOUTH APPRENTICESHIP PROJECT (1993) *Youth Apprenticeship and School-to-Work Transition in California: Statewide Conference Bulletin*, Sacramento, CA: Author.

CAMPBELL, P.B. and BASINGER, K.S. (1985) *Economic and Non-economic Effects of Alternative Transitions Through School to Work*, Columbus, OH: The National Center for Research in Vocational Education, Ohio State University.

CAMPBELL, P.B., ELLIOT, J., LAUGHLIN, S. and SEUSY, E. (1987) *The Dynamics of Vocational Education Efforts on Labor Market Outcomes*, Columbus, OH: The National Center for Research in Vocational Education, Ohio State University.

CANTOR, J.A. (1988) *Naval Shipyard Apprentice Program and Community-Technical College Linkages: A Model for Success. Conference Paper*, (ERIC Document ED 308 890).

CANTOR, J.A. (1991) 'The auto industry's new model: Car companies and community colleges collaborate to provide high-technology training', *Vocational Education Journal*, 66, 7, pp. 26–9.

CANTOR, J.A. (1992) *Apprenticeship and Community Colleges: Collaborations for Tomorrow's Workforce. Final Report*, Bronx, NY: Lehman College, City University of New York.

CAPPELLI, P. (1992) *Is the 'Skills Gap' Really about Attitudes?*, Philadelphia, PA: National Center on the Educational Quality of the Workforce.

CARNEVALE, A.P. *et al.* (1988) *Workplace Basics: The Skills Employers Want*, Alexandria, VA: The American Society for Training and Development.

CARNEVALE, A.P. (1991) *America and the New Economy*, US Department of Labor, Employment and Training Administration, Alexandria, VA: The American Society for Training and Development.

CARROLL, D.C. and CHAN-KOPKA, T.L. (1988) *College Students Who Work: 1980–84 Analysis Findings from High School and Beyond*, Washington, DC: National Center for Education Statistics, (ERIC Document No. ED 297 680).

CASNER-LOTTO, J. (1988) *Successful Training Strategies*, San Francisco, CA: Jossey-Bass.

CAVE, G. and DOOLITTLE, F. (1991) *Assessing Jobstart*, New York: Manpower Demonstration Research Corporation.

CAVE, G. and QUINT, J. (1990) *Career Beginnings Impact Evaluation: Findings from a Program for Disadvantaged High School Students*, New York: Manpower Demonstration Research Corporation.

CHARNER, I. and FRASER, B.S. (1987) *Youth and Work: What We Know, What We Don't Know, What We Need To Know*, Washington, DC: William T. Grant Foundation.

CHEW, C. (1992) *Tech Prep and Counseling*, Madison: Center on Education and Work, University of Wisconsin.

CHOY, S.P. and HORN, L.J. (1992) *A Guide to Using Post-secondary Transcript Data and an Overview of Course-Taking in Less-than-Four-Year Post-secondary Institutions*, Berkeley, CA: National Center for Research in Vocational Education, University of California.

CHUNG, Y. (1990) 'Educated mis-employment in Hong Kong: Earnings effects of employment in unmatched fields of work', *Economics of Education Review*, 9, 4, pp. 343–50.

COMMITTEE FOR ECONOMIC DEVELOPMENT (1985) *Investing in Our Children*, New York: Committee for Economic Development.

CONKLIN, D. (1987) 'Corporation-community college partnerships: High technology apprenticeship training', paper delivered at the annual meeting of the American Educational Research Association Washington, DC: April, (ERIC Document No. ED 306 982)

CRAIN, R.L., HEEBNER, A.L. and SI, Y-P. (1992) *The Effectiveness of New York City's Career Magnet Schools: An Evaluation of Ninth Grade Performance Using An Experimental Design*, National Center for Research in Vocational Education, Publication No. MDS-173, April.

CRAWFORD, E. and ROMERO, C. (1991) *A Changing Nation — Its Changing Labor Force*, Washington, DC: National Commission for Employment Policy.

CROCKETT, L. and SMINK, J. (1991) *The Mentoring Guidebook: A Practical Guide for Designing and Managing a Mentoring Program*, Clemson, SC: National Dropout Prevention Center.

CROW, D., HUTCHINSON, J.R., GERNHART, Z. and BUAN, C.M. (1987) *A Step-by-Step Guide to Integrating Science Concepts and Vocational Skills in the High School Classroom: The Sandy Union High School Experience*, Clearing, No. 47, pp. 18–22, January/February.

D'AMICO, R. (1984) 'Does employment during high school impair academic progress?', *Sociology of Education*, 57, 3, pp. 152–64.

D'AMICO, R. and MAXWELL, N. (1990) *Black-White Employment Differences during the School-to-Work Transition: An Explanation for between- and within-Race Differences*, Palo Alto, CA: SRI International.

DAWSON, J.D. (1989) 'Educational outcomes for students in cooperative education', *Journal of Cooperative Education*, 25, 2, pp. 6–13.

DAYTON, C. (1988) *Jobs for the Disadvantages' Graduate Follow-up Survey*, Policy Analysis for California Education (PACE), Policy Paper No. pp. 88–5–6, May.

DAYTON, C. and WEISBERG, A. (1987) *School-to-Work and Academy Demonstration Programs: 1986–87 Evaluation Report*, Policy Analysis for California Education (PACE), Policy Paper No. PC87–11–12-EMCF, November.

DORNSIFE, C. (1992) *Beyond Articulation: The Development of Tech Prep Programs*, Berkeley, CA: The National Center for Research in Vocational Education, University of California.

DRISCOLL, F.G. (1986) *Project COFFEE: Cooperative Federation for Educational Experiences*, submission prepared for the Joint Dissemination Review Panel, Oxford Public Schools.

EHRENBERG, R.G. and SHERMAN, D.R. (1987) 'Employment while in college: Academic achievement and post-college outcomes', *Journal of Human Resources*, 22, 1, pp. 1–23.

EIDE, K. (1979) 'Education and work: Discord and harmony' in *Learning and Working, a Prospects Report*, UNESCO, pp. 89–101.

ELLWOOD, D. (1982) 'Teenage unemployment: Permanent scars or temporary blemishes?' in FREEMAN, R.B. and WISE, D.A. (Eds) *The Youth Labor Market Problem*, University of Chicago Press.

EVALUATION AND TRAINING INSTITUTE (1991) *Longitudinal Evaluation of 2 + 2 Career-Vocational Education Articulation Projects. First Year Interim Report*, Sacramento, California: California Community Colleges, (ERIC Document No. ED 335 467).

FARKAS, G., HOTCHKISS, L. and STROMSDORFER, E.W. (1988) 'Vocational training, supply constraints, and individual economic outcomes', paper presented at the annual meeting of the American Educational Research Association, New Orleans, April.

FARLAND, R. and ANDERSON, B. (1988) *Apprenticeship Related and Supplemental Instruction*, Sacramento, CA: California Community Colleges, Office of the Chancellor, (ERIC Document ED 301 278).

FINKELSTEIN N. and LATTING J. (forthcoming) 'The prevalence of youth apprenticeship programs in the United States', paper prepared for the National Assessment of Vocational Education.

FLAXMAN, E., ASCHER, C. and HARRINGTON, C. (1988) *Mentoring Programs and Practices: An Analysis of the Literature*, New York: Institute for Urban and Minority Education, Teachers College, Columbia University.

FLETCHER, J.K. (1988) 'The correlation of GPA to co-op work performance of business undergraduates', *Journal of Cooperative Education*, 25, 1, pp. 44–52.

FLETCHER, J.K. (1989) 'Student outcomes: What do we know and how do we know it?', *Journal of Cooperative Education*, 26, 1, pp. 26–38.

FLYNN, P.M. (1985) *The Impact of Technological Change on Jobs and Workers*, Washington, DC: Employment Training Administration, US Department of Labor.

FREEDMAN, M. (1991) *The Kindness of Strangers: Reflections on the Mentoring Movement*, Philadelphia, PA: Public/Private Ventures.

FREEDMAN, M. and JAFFE, N. (1992) 'Elder mentors: Giving schools a hand', *NASSP Bulletin*, 76, 549, pp. 22–28.

FREEMAN, R.B. (1974) 'Occupational training in proprietary schools and technical institutes', *Review of Economics and Statistics*, 56, 3, pp. 310–8.

FREEMAN, R.B. (1991) 'Labor market tightness and the mismatch between demand and supply of less-educated young men in the United States in the 1980s' in PADOA-SCHIOPPA, F. (Ed) *Mismatch and Labor Mobility*, New York and Cambridge: Cambridge University Press.

FRENCH RIVER EDUCATION CENTER (1989) *Strategies for Educating the At-Risk Student: Project Coffee, JOBS*, North Oxford, MA.

FULLAN, M. (1991) *The New Meaning of Educational Change*, New York: Teachers College Press.

FULLAN, M. (1992) *Successful School Improvement*, Buckingham: Open University Press.

FULLERTON, H.N., JR. (1989) 'New labor force projections, spanning 1988 to 2000', *Monthly Labor Review*, November.

GAMBONE, M.A. (1993) *Strengthening Programs for Youth: Promoting*

Adolescent Development in the JTPA System, Philadelphia, PA: Public/Private Ventures.

GIULIANO, V. (1982) 'The mechanization of office work', *Scientific American*, 247, 3.

GOLDBERGER, S. (1993) *Creating an American-Style Youth Apprenticeship Program: The Formative Evaluation of Project Pro Tech*, Cambridge, MA: Jobs for the Future.

GOLDBERGER, S., KAZIS, R. and O'FLANAGAN, M.K. (1994) *Learning Through Work: Designing and Implementing Quality Worksite Learning for High School Students*, New York: Manpower Demonstration Research Corporation.

GOLDSTEIN, M.B. (1991) 'The impacts of teenage employment: Teachers' perceptions versus student realities', Paper presented at the annual convention of the American Psychological Association, San Francisco, 16–20 August (ERIC Document No. ED 335 609).

GOODWIN, D. (1989) *Post-secondary Vocational Education. Volume IV, Final Report of the National Assessment of Vocational Education*, Washington, DC: US Department of Education.

GRAY, K. and HUANG, N.T. (1992) 'Tech prep: Will it pay?', *Journal of Industrial Teacher Education*.

GREENBERGER, E. and STEINBERG, L. (1986) *When Teenagers Work: The Psychological and Social Costs of Adolescent Employment*, New York: Basic Books.

GREIM, J. (1992) *Adult/Youth Relationships Pilot Project. Initial Implementation Report*, Philadelphia, PA: Public/Private Ventures.

CROSSMAN, G.M., WARMBROD, C.P. and KURTH, P.K. (1988) *Post-secondary Cooperative Education: An Examination of Survey Results and Policy Implications*, Columbus, OH: National Center for Research in Vocational Education, Ohio State University, (ERIC Document No. ED 309 294).

GRUBB, W.N. (1990) *The Economic Returns to Post-secondary Education: New Evidence from the National Longitudinal Study of the Class of 1972*, Berkeley, CA: School of Education, University of California.

GRUBB, W.N. (1991a) *The Effects of Post-secondary Education on Access to Occupations*, Berkeley, CA: School of Education, University of California.

GRUBB, W.N. (1991b) *The Long-Run Effects of Proprietary Schools on Wages and Earnings: Implications for Federal Policy*, Berkeley, CA: School of Education, University of California.

GRUBB, W.N. (1992a) 'Post-secondary vocational education and the sub-baccalaureate labor market: New evidence on economic returns', *Economics of Education Review*, 11, 3.

GRUBB, W.N. (1992b) 'The varied economic returns to post-secondary education: New evidence from the Class of 1972', *Journal of Human Resources*.

GRUBB, W.N. (1993a) 'Further tests of screening on education and observed ability', *Economics of Education Review*, 12, pp. 125–36.

GRUBB, W.N. (1993b) *The Economic Effects of Sub-baccalaureate Education: Corrections and Extensions*, Berkeley, CA: School of Education, University of California. Draft, November.

GRUBB, W.N., BROWN, C., KAUFMAN, P. and LEDERER, J. (1990) *Order Amidst Complexity: The Status of Coordination Among Vocational Education, Job Training Partnership Act, and Welfare-to-Work Programs*, Berkeley, CA: National Center for Research in Vocational Education, University of California, Document MDS-063.

GRUBB, W.N., DAVIS, G., PLIHAL, J. and LUM, J. (1991) *The Cunning Hand, The Cultured Mind: Models for Integrating Vocational and Academic Education*, Berkeley, CA: National Center for Research in Vocational Education, University of California, Document MDS-141.

GRUBB, W.N. and STASZ, C. (1992) *Assessing the Integration of Academic and Vocational Education: Methods and Questions, Working Paper*, Berkeley, CA: National Center for Research in Vocational Education, University of California.

HAFER, A.A. (1982) *Career Planning and Development Programs for Two-Year Colleges*, (ERIC Document No. ED 219 522).

HAHN, A. and LERMAN, R. (1985) *What Works in Youth Employment Policy?* Washington, DC: National Planning Association.

HAMILTON, S.F. (1990) *Apprenticeship for Adulthood: Preparing Youth for the Future*, New York: Free Press.

HAMILTON, S.F. (1993) 'Prospects for an American-style youth apprenticeship system', *Educational Researcher*, 22, pp. 11–16.

HAMILTON, S.F. and HAMILTON, M.A. (1990) *Linking Up: Final Report on a Mentoring Program for Youth*, Ithaca, NY: Department of Human Development and Family Studies, Cornell University.

HAMILTON, S.F. and POWERS, J.L. (1990) 'Failed expectations: Working-class girls' transition from school to work', *Youth and Society*, 22, 2, pp. 241–62.

HAMMES, J. and HALLER, E. (1983) 'Making ends meet: Some of the consequences of part-time work for college students', *Journal of College Student Personnel*, pp. 529–35.

HAMMONS, F. (1992) 'The first step in tech prep program evaluation: The identification of program performance indicators', unpublished dissertation, Blasksburg, VA: Virginia Polytechnic Institute and State University.

HARP, L. (1993) 'SREB project helps schools blur line between vocational and academic tracks', *Education Week*, 23 June, p. 8.

HARRIS, L. and ASSOCIATES (1991) 'Poll on young people's skills', *San Francisco Chronicle*, 30 September, p. A3.

HASHIMOTO, M. and RAISIAN, J. (1985) 'Employment tenures and earnings profiles in Japan and the United States', *American Economic Review*, September, pp. 716–24.

HAY, J.E., EVANS, K. and LINDSAY, C.A. (1970) 'Student part-time jobs: Relevant or non-relevant? *Vocational Guidance Quarterly*, pp. 113–8.

HAYWARD, B.J. (1991) 'Dropout prevention demonstration projects: Factors that affect implementation and effectiveness', paper presented at the annual meeting of the American Educational Research Association, Chicago, April.

HAYWARD, B.J. (1992) 'Dropout prevention in vocational education: Findings from the first two years of the demonstration', paper presented at the annual meeting of the American Educational Research Association, San Francisco, April.

HAYWARD, B.J., ADELMAN, N.E. and APLING, R.N. (1988) *Exemplary Secondary Vocational Education: An Exploratory Study Of Seven Programs, Discussion Papers for the National Assessment of Vocational Education*, Washington, DC: US Department of Education.

HAYWARD, B.J. TALLMADGE, G. and LEU, D. (1992) *Evaluation of Dropout Prevention and Reentry Demonstration Projects in Vocational Education, Final Report: Phase II, Revised Draft*, Research Triangle Institute.

HECKMAN, J.J. (1979) 'Sample selection bias as a specification error', *Econometrica*, 47, 1, pp. 153–61.

HEERMAN, B. (1975) *Cooperative Education in Community Colleges*, San Francisco, CA: Jossey-Bass.

HEINEMANN, H.N. (1988) 'Cooperative education in the community college', *Journal of Cooperative Education*, 24, 2–3, pp. 47–60.

HERRNSTADT, I.L., HOROWITZ, M.A. and SUM, A. (1979) *The Transition from School to Work: The Contribution of Cooperative Education Programs at the Secondary Level*, Boston, MA: Department of Economics, Northeastern University.

HIRSCHHORN, L. (1984) *Beyond Mechanization: Work and Technology in a Postindustrial Age*, Cambridge, MA: MIT Press.

HIRSHBERG, D. (1991) *The Role of the Community College in Economic and Workforce Development*, ERIC Digest, No. ED0-JC-91-05, (ERIC Document No. ED 339 443).

HOERNER, J., CLOWES, D. and IMPARA, J. (1992) *Identification and Dissemination of Articulated Tech Prep Practices for At-Risk Students.*

Berkeley, CA: National Center for Research in Vocational Education, University of California.

HOLLENBECK, K. (1992) 'Post-secondary education as triage: The consequences of post-secondary education tracks on wages, earnings and wage growth', paper presented at the Western Economics Association meetings, San Francisco.

HOPKINS, C., STERN, D., STONE, J.R. and McMILLION, M. (1989) 'Learning from school-based experience programs', paper presented at the annual meeting of the American Educational Research Association, San Francisco, April.

HORN, R. (1989) 'Economic outcomes of postsecondary vocational training', in GOODWIN, D. (Ed) *Final Report. Volume IV: Postsecondary Vocational Education, National Assessment of Vocational Education*, Washington, DC: US Department of Education, pp. 51–71.

HOTCHKISS, L. (1986) 'Work and schools: Complements or competitors?' in BORMAN, K. and REISMAN, J. (Eds) *Becoming a Worker*, Norword, NJ: Ablex, p. 90–115.

HOTCHKISS, L. (1987) *Non-economic Effects of Vocational Education*, Columbus, OH: National Center for Research in Vocational Education, Ohio State University.

HOYT, K.B. (1991) 'A proposal for making transition from schooling to employment an important component of educational reform', *Future Choices*, 2, 2, pp. 73–86.

HULL, D. and PARNELL, D. (1991) *Tech Prep Associate Degree: A Win/Win Experience,* Waco, TX: Center for Occupational Research and Development.

HULL, W. (1987) *Comprehensive model for planning and evaluation of secondary vocational education programs in Georgia,* Atlanta: Georgia State Department of Education, (ERIC Document Reproduction Service No. ED 284 983).

JAMIESON, I., MILLER, A. and WATTS, A.G. (1988) *Mirrors of Work: Work Simulations in Schools.* London: Falmer Press.

JOBS FOR THE FUTURE (1991) *Essential Elements of Youth Apprenticeship Programs: A Preliminary Outline.* Cambridge, MA: Jobs for the Future.

JOBS FOR THE FUTURE (1993a) *Learning that Works: A Youth Apprenticeship Briefing Book,* Cambridge, MA: Jobs for the Future.

JOBS FOR THE FUTURE (1993b) *Student Apprenticeship News, Number 6,* Cambridge, MA: Jobs for the Future.

JOHNSTON, W.B. *et al.* (1987) *Workforce 2000: Work and Workers for the 21st Century,* Indianapolis, IN: Hudson Institute.

KANE, T.J. and ROUSE, C.E. (1992) *Labor Market Returns to Community*

College, Cambridge, MA: John F. Kennedy School of Government, Harvard University.

KATZ, L.F. and MURPHY, K.M. (1992) 'Changes in relative wages, 1963–1987: Supply and demand factors', *Quarterly Journal of Economics*, February.

KAZIS, R. and BARTON, P.E. (1993) *Improving the Transition from School to Work in the United States*, Washington DC: American Youth Policy Forum, Competitiveness Policy Council, Jobs for the Future.

KAZIS, R. and ROCHE, B. (1991) *New US Initiatives for the Transition from School to Work. Occasional Paper No. 8*, Geneva: International Labour Office.

KEARNS, D.T. and DOYLE, D.P. (1988) *Winning the Brain Race: A Bold Plan to Make Our Schools Competitive*, San Francisco, CA: Institute for Contemporary Studies.

KERKA, S. (1991) *Cooperative Education: Characteristics and Effectiveness, ERIC Digest No. 91*, (ERIC Document No. ED 312 455).

KIRSCH, I.S. and JUNGEBLUT, A. (1986) *Literacy: Profiles of America's Young Adults. Final Report*, Princeton, NJ: National Assessment of Educational Progress.

KNAPP, M.R. (1989) 'Alaska's young entrepreneurs', *Vocational Education Journal*, November/December, pp. 40–1.

KOHEN, A., NESTEL, G. and KARMAS, C. (1978) 'Factors affecting individual persistence rates in undergraduate college programs', *American Educational Research Journal*, 15, pp. 233–51.

KOMINSKI, R. (1990) *'What's It Worth? Educational Background and Economic Status: Spring 1987*, Washington, DC: US Department of Commerce, Bureau of the Census.

KREBS, U.H. (1988) 'Usefulness of the co-op experience: A study of community college students', *Journal of Cooperative Education*, 24, 1, pp. 32–42.

LAH, D. *et al.* (1983) *Longer-Term Impacts of Pre-Employment Services on the Employment and Earnings of Disadvantaged Youth: A Project of the Private Sector Initiatives Demonstration of Public/Private Ventures*, Philadelphia, PA: Public/Private Ventures.

LALONDE, R.J. (1986) 'Evaluating the econometric evaluations of training programs with experimental data', *American Economic Review*, 65, 4, pp. 604–620.

LAUR-ERNST, U. (1992) 'The dual system in Germany — Advantages of cooperative models of vocational training' in *Schools and Industry: Partners for a Quality Education*, Proceedings of an EC/US conference held in Noordwijk, The Netherlands, The Hague: Nuffic publishers.

LAYCOCK, A.B., HERMON, M.V. and LAETZ, V. (1992) 'Cooperative education: Key factors related to a quality experience', *Journal of Cooperative Education,* 27, 3, pp. 36–46.

LAYTON, J. and BRAGG, D. (1992) 'Initiation of tech prep by the fifty states' in BRAGG D. (Ed) *Implementing Tech Prep: A Guide to Planning a Quality Initiative,* Berkeley, CA: National Center for Research in Vocational Education, University of California.

LAZERSON, M. and GRUBB, W.N. (1974) *American Education and Vocationalism: A Documentary History,* New York: Teachers College Press.

LERMAN, R.I. and POUNCY, H. (1990) 'The compelling case for youth apprenticeships', *The Public Interest,* 101, pp. 62–77.

LESKE, G. and PERSICO, J., JR. (1984) *Indicators of Quality in Cooperative Education; A Review and Synthesis of Research,* St. Paul: Minnesota Research and Development Center for Vocational Education, Department of Vocational and Technical Education, University of Minnesota.

LEVIN, H.M. and RUMBERGER, R.W. (1983) 'Secondary education in an age of high technology', *NASSP Bulletin,* 67, 467, pp. 49–55.

LEVY, F. and MURNANE, R.J. (1992) 'US earnings levels and earnings inequality: A review of recent trends and proposed explanations', *Journal of Economic Literature* 30, September, pp. 1333–81.

LEWIS, M. (1988) 'A commentary on C. Parsons: The Bridge-Cooperative education for all high school students' in William T. Grant Foundation *Youth and America's Future,* pp. 86–90.

LEWIS, M.V., GARDNER, J.A. and SEITZ, P. (1983) *High School Work Experience and Its Effects,* Columbus, OH: National Center for Research in Vocational Education, Ohio State University.

LILLYDAHL, J.H. (1990) 'Academic achievement and part-time employment of high school students', *Journal of Economic Education,* summer, pp. 307–16.

LISTON, E.J. (1986) *The CCRI Electric Boat Program: A Partnership for Progress in Economic Development. Conference Paper,* (ERIC Document No. ED 275 373).

LISTON, E.J. and WARD, C.V. (1984) 'The greenhouse effect', *Community and Junior College Journal,* 55, 3, pp. 20–3.

LONG, J., WARMBROD, C., FADDIS, C. and LERNER, M. (1986) *Avenues for Articulation: Coordinating Secondary and Post-secondary Programs,* Columbus, OH: National Center for Research in Vocational Education, Ohio State University.

LYKE, R., GABE, T. and ALEMAN, S.R. (1991) *Early Labor Market Experiences of Proprietary School Students,* Washington, DC: Congressional Research Service, The Library of Congress.

Lynch, L.M. (1989) 'The Youth labor market in the eighties: Determinants of re-employment probabilities for young men and women', *Review of Economics and Statistics*, 71, 1, pp. 37–45.

Lynch, L.M. (1992) 'Private-sector training and the earnings of young workers', *American Economic Review*, 82, 1, pp. 299–312.

Maddala, G.S. (1983) *Limited-Dependent and Qualitative Variables in Econometrics*, Cambridge, UK: Cambridge University Press.

Manely, K.K., et al. (1986) *An Assessment of the Training Needs of Career-Vocational Counselors, Job Placement and Career Resource Center Personnel in Michigan: Implications for Long-Term Professional Development. Final Report*, Big Rapids, MI: Center for Occupational Education, Ferris State College.

Manpower Demonstration Research Corporation (1980) *Summary and Findings of the National Supported Work Demonstration*, Cambridge, MA: Ballinger Publishing.

Marsh, H.W. (1991) 'Employment during high school: Character building or a subversion of academic goals?', *Sociology of Education*, 64 July, pp. 172–89.

McDonald's Youth Apprenticeship Program (1993) *Briefing Report*, Cambridge, MA: Jobs for the Future.

McKinney, F., Fields, E., Kurth, P. and Kelly, F. (1988) *Factors Influencing the Success of Secondary/Post-secondary Vocational-Technical Education Articulation Programs*, Columbus, OH: National Center for Research in Vocational Education, Ohio State University.

Medrich, E.A. and Vergun, R. (1994) *Earnings and Employment Outcomes for Post-secondary Degree Holders in Vocational Subject Areas*, Berkeley, CA: MPR Associates.

Meyer, R.H. and Wise, D.A. (1982) 'High school preparation and early labor force experience', in Freeman, R.B. and Wise, D.A. (Eds) *The Youth Labor Market Problem*, Chicago, IL: University of Chicago Press.

Miller, A., Watts, A.G. and Jamieson, I (1991) *Rethinking Work Experience*, London: Falmer Press.

Mincer, J. (1974) *Schooling, Experience, and Earnings*, New York: Columbia University Press.

Mincer, J. and Higuchi, Y. (1988) 'Wage structures and labor turnover in the US and Japan, *Journal of the Japanese and International Economies*, June, pp. 97–133.

Mitchell, V., Russell, E. and Benson, C. 1990 *Exemplary Urban Career-Oriented Secondary School Programs*, Berkeley, CA: National Center for Research in Vocational Education, University of California, Document Number MDS-012.

MOLONEY, T.W. and MCKAUGHAN, M. (1990) *New Commonwealth Fund Findings on the Benefits of mentoring; 400 Mentors and 400 High School Students Interviewed, Commonwealth Fund Press Release*, 27 March.

MONK-TURNER, E. (1986) 'Wage differences between community and four-year college entrants', *Free Inquiry in Creative Sociology*, 14, 2, pp. 149–51.

MORTIMER, J.T. and FINCH, M.D. (1986) 'The effects of part-time work on adolescent self-concept and achievement', in BORMAN, K.M. and REISMAN, J. (Eds) *Becoming a Worker*, Norwood, NJ: Ablex Publishing.

MORTIMER, J.T., RYU, S., DENNEHY, K. and LEE, C. (1992) 'Part-time work and occupational value formation in adolescence', paper presented at the annual meeting of the American Sociological Association.

MORTIMER, J.T., SHANAHAN, M. and RYU, S. (1991) 'The effects of adolescent employment on school-related orientation and behavior', in SILBEREREISEN, K. and TODT, E. (Eds) *Adolescence in Context: The Interplay of Family, School, Peers and Work in Adjustment*, Minneapolis, MN: University of Minnesota.

MUHA, S., *et al.* (1988) *Redesigning College Job Placement for the 1990s*, Austin: Coordinating Board, Texas College and University System, (ERIC Document No. ED 300 058).

MURNANE, R.J., WILLETT, J.B. and LEVY, F. (1992) *The Growing Importance of Cognitive Skills in Wage Determination*, Cambridge, MA: Harvard Graduate School of Education.

NATIONAL ACADEMY OF SCIENCES (1984) *High Schools and the Changing Workplace: The Employers' View. Panel on Secondary School Education and the Changing Workplace*, Washington, DC: National Academy Press.

NATIONAL ACADEMY OF SCIENCES (1986) *Human Resource Practices for Implementing Advanced Manufacturing Technology. Committee on the Effective Implementation of Advanced Manufacturing Technology*, Washington, DC: National Academy Press.

NATIONAL ALLIANCE OF BUSINESS (1992) *Real Jobs for Real People: An Employer's Guide to Youth Apprenticeship*, Washington, DC: National Alliance of Business.

NATIONAL CENTER ON EDUCATION AND THE ECONOMY (1990) *America's Choice: High Skills or Low Wages!*, Rochester, NY: National Center on Education and the Economy.

NATIONAL CENTER ON THE EDUCATIONAL QUALITY OF THE WORKFORCE (1992) *A Crosswalk of National Data Sets Focusing on Worker Training*, Philadelphia, PA: University of Pennsylvania.

NATIONAL CHILD LABOR COMMITTEE (1984) *Keys to Cooperative Education Programs. Volume II*, New York: National Child Labor Committee.

NATIONAL COMMISSION ON SECONDARY VOCATIONAL EDUCATION (1984) *The Unfinished Agenda: The Role of Occupational Education in the High School*, Washington, DC: Office of Vocational and Adult Education, (ERIC Document No. ED 251 622).

NATIONAL COUNCIL FOR OCCUPATIONAL EDUCATION (1989) *Occupational Program Articulation: A Report of a Study Prepared by the Task Force on Occupational Program Articulation*, Wausau, WI: National Council for Occupational Education, (ERIC Document No. ED 321 795).

NATIONAL COUNCIL ON EXCELLENCE IN EDUCATION (1983) *A Nation at Risk*, Washington, DC: GPO.

NATIONAL COUNCIL ON VOCATIONAL EDUCATION (1991) *Occupational Competencies: A Study of the Vocational Education Needs of the Manufacturing and Aviation Maintenance Industries*, Berkeley, CA.

NATIONAL INSTITUTE OF EDUCATION (1981) *The Vocational Education Study, Final Report*, Washington, DC: National Institute of Education.

NATIONAL YOUTH EMPLOYMENT COALITION (1992) *Making Sense of Federal Job Training Policy*, Washington, DC: National Youth Employment Coalition and William T. Grant Foundation Commission on Youth and America's Future.

NEUMAN, S. and ZIDERMAN, A. (1991) 'Vocational schooling, occupational matching, and labor market earnings in Israel', *Journal of Human Resources*, 26, 2, pp. 256–81.

NEW YORK STATE EDUCATION DEPARTMENT (1990) *Where Do All the Students Go? A Statewide Follow-Up Survey of Secondary Students Completing Occupational Education Programs at School Districts and BOCES*, Division of Occupational Education Programs, Albany, NY: New York State Education Department, (ERIC Document Reproduction Service No. ED 333 104).

NOTHDURFT, W.E. (1990) *Youth Apprenticeship, American Style: A Strategy for Expanding School and Career Opportunities*, Washington, DC: Consortium on Youth Apprenticeship.

ORGANIZATION FOR ECONOMIC COOPERATION AND DEVELOPMENT (1993) *Employment Outlook*, July, Paris: Organization for Economic Cooperation and Development.

ORGANIZATION FOR ECONOMIC COOPERATION AND DEVELOPMENT (1994) *Employment/Unemployment Study, Draft Background Report*, SG/EUS(94)8, Paris: Organization for Economic Cooperation and Development.

ORR, M.T. (1987) *Keeping Students in School: A Guide to Effective Drop-*

out Prevention Programs and Services, San Francisco, CA: Jossey-Bass.

OSTERMAN, P. (1980) *Getting Started*, Cambridge, MA: MIT Press.

OSTERMAN, P. (1989) 'The job market for adolescents', in STERN, D. and EICHORN, D. (Eds) *Adolescence and Work*, Hillsdale, NJ: Lawrence Erlbaum.

OSTERMAN, P. (1991) *Is There a Problem with the Youth Labor Market and If So How Should We Fix It?: Lessons for the US from American and European Experience*, draft.

OWENS, T.J. (1992) 'Where do we go from here? Post-high school choices of American men', *Youth and Society*, 23, 4, pp. 452–77.

PARMERLEE-GREINER, G. (1993) 'Job placement counseling, and on-site child care', *Journal for Vocational and Special Needs*, 15, 2, pp. 26–30.

PARNELL, D. (1985) *The Neglected Majority*, Washington, DC: Community College Press.

PARSONS, C. (1988) *The Bridge: Cooperative Education for All High School Students*, Washington, DC: William T. Grant Foundation.

PAULY, E., KOPP, H. and HAIMSON, J. (1994) *Home-Grown Lessons: Innovative Programs Linking Work and High School*, New York: Manpower Demonstration Research Corporation.

PORTLAND COMMUNITY COLLEGE (1991) *Women in Education for Apprenticeship and Non-Traditional Employment. Final Performance Report*, (ERIC Document No. ED 331 994).

PSACHAROPOULOS, G. (1987) 'To vocationalize or not to vocationalize? That is the curriculum question', *International Review of Education*, 33, 2, pp. 187–211.

PUCKETT, J.L. (1986) 'Foxfire reconsidered: A critical ethnohistory of a twenty-year experiment in progressive education', doctoral dissertation, University of North Carolina at Chapel Hill.

RAIZEN, S.A. (1989) *Reforming Education for Work: A Cognitive Science Perspective*, Berkeley, CA: National Center for Research in Vocational Education, University of California.

RAMER, M. (1991) *Community College/High School Articulation in California: 2 + 2 Program Definition and Barriers to Implementation*, Sacramento: California Community College Administrators for Occupational Education.

REAL ENTERPRISES (1989) *Georgia REAL Enterprises: Rural Entrepreneurship Through Action Learning*, Atlanta: REAL Enterprises.

REICH, R. (1993) *Youth Apprenticeship and Lifelong Learning: Some Preliminary Notions*, Washington, DC: US Department of Labor, Office of Information, 22 February.

References

REISNER, E.R. (1989) *A Review of Programs Involving College Students as Tutors or Mentors in Grades K-12*, Washington, DC: Policy Studies Associates, Inc.

RESNICK, L.B. (1987a) 'Learning in school and out', *Educational Researcher*, 16, pp. 13–20.

RESNICK, L.B. (1987b) *Education and Learning to Think*, Washington, DC: National Academy Press.

RICKS, F., VAN GYN, G., BRANTON, G., CUT, J., LOKEN, M. and NEY, T. (1991) 'Theory and research in cooperative education: Practice implications', *Journal of Cooperative Education*, 27, 1, pp. 7–20.

RIDING, A. (1993) 'Europe's young: Hope amid joblessness, and ideals alongside anger', *International Herald Tribune*, 13 August, p. 2.

RODITI, H.F. (1991) *How Much Does a Youth Apprenticeship Program Cost, and Who Will Pay for It? Lessons from Some Long-Standing School-to-Work Programs and Youth Apprenticeship Programs under Development*, Cambridge, MA: Jobs for the Future, Inc.

ROSENBAUM, J. (Ed) (1992) *Youth Apprenticeship in America: Guidelines for Building an Effective System*, Washington, DC: William T. Grant Foundation Commission on Work, Family, and Citizenship.

ROWE, P.M. (1989) 'Employer expectations of future requirements for cooperative education students', *Journal of Cooperative Education*, 25, 1, pp. 53–8.

ROWE, P.M. (1990) 'Entry differences between students in cooperative and regular programs', *Journal of Cooperative Education*, 26, 1, pp. 16–25.

RUHM, C. (1993) *Is High School Employment Consumption or Investment?* Greensboro, NC: Department of Economics, University of North Carolina.

RUMBERGER, R.W. and DAYMONT, T.N. (1984) 'The economic value of academic and vocational training acquired in high school', in BORUS, M.E. (Ed) *Youth and the Labor Market: Analyses of the National Longitudinal Survey*, Kalamazoo, MI: Upjohn Institute.

SAN, G. (1986) 'The early labor force experience of college students and their post-college success', *Economics of Education Review*, 5, 1, pp. 65–76.

SCHILL, W.J., McCARTIN, R. and MEYER, K. (1985) 'Youth employment: Its relationship to academic and family variables', *Journal of Vocational Behavior*, 26, pp. 155–63.

SIEDENBERG, J.M. (1989a) 'Incorporating cooperative education into human capital theory: A solution to the student benefit dillema', *Journal of Cooperative Education*, 25, 1, pp. 8–15.

Siedenberg, J.M. (1989b) 'Isolating co-op as a predictor of monetary rewards: An economist's view', *Journal of Cooperative Education*, 25, 3, pp. 8–15.

Siedenberg, J.M. (1990) 'A "come-from-behind" victory for cooperative education', *Journal of Cooperative Education*, 27, 1, pp. 21–37.

Silvestri, G. and Lukasiewicz, J. (1989) 'Projections of occupational employment, 1988–2000', *Monthly Labor Review*, November.

Skinner, N. (1990) *Forming the Future with a Unique Partnership, Conference Paper*, (ERIC Document No. 328 706).

Somers, G.M. (1989) 'Model for analysis of co-op wages', *Journal of Cooperative Education*, 25, 3, pp. 66–78.

Stanwyck, D.J. and Anson, C.A. (1989) *The Adopt-A-Student Evaluation Project: Final Report*, Atlanta, GA: Department of Educational Foundations, Georgia State University.

Stasz, C., Kaganoff, T. and Eden, R. (1993) 'Integrating academic and vocational education: A review of the literature,' paper prepared for the National Assessment of Vocational Education, National Center for Research in Vocational Education, University of California, Berkeley.

Steedman, H. (1993) 'The economics of youth training in Germany', *The Economic Journal*, 103, pp. 1279–91.

Steel, L. (1991) 'Early work experience among white and non-white youths; Implications for subsequent enrollment and employment', *Youth and Society*, 22, 4, pp. 419–47.

Steinberg, L.D. (1982) 'Jumping off the work experience bandwagon', *Journal of Youth and Adolescence*, 11, pp. 183–205.

Steinberg, L.D. (1991) 'The logic of adolescence' in Edelman, O. and Ladner, J. (Eds) *Adolescence and Poverty: Challenge for the 1990's*, Washington, DC: Center for National Policy Studies.

Steinberg, L.D. and Dornbusch, S.M. (1991) 'Negative correlates of part-time employment during adolescence: Replication and elaboration', *Developmental Psychology*, 27, 2, pp. 304–13.

Steinberg, L.D., Fegley, S. and Dornbusch, S.M. (1993) 'Negative impact of part-time work on adolescent adjustment: Evidence from a longitudinal study', *Developmental Psychology*, 29, 2.

Stephenson, S.P., Jr. (1981) 'In-school labour force status and post-school wage rates of young men', *Applied Economics*, 13, pp. 279–302.

Stephenson, S.P., Jr. (1982) 'Work in college and subsequent wage rates', *Research in Higher Education*, 17, pp. 165–78.

Stern, D. (1984) 'School-based enterprise and the quality of work experience: A study of high school students,' *Youth and Society*, 15, 4, pp. 401–27.

STERN, D. (1990) *Combining School and Work: Options in High Schools and Two-Year Colleges*, Washington, DC: Office of Vocational and Adult Education, US Department of Education.

STERN, D. (1992a) 'School-to-work programs and services in secondary schools and two-year public post-secondary institutions', paper prepared for the National Assessment of Vocational Education, Berkeley, CA: School of Education, University of California.

STERN, D. (1992b) 'Economic returns to non-baccalaureate education and training for post-secondary students and adults', paper prepared for the Committee on Post-secondary Education and Training for the Workplace, National Research Council/National Academy of Sciences, Berkeley, CA: School of Education, University of California.

STERN, D., DAYTON, C., PAIK, I. and WEISBERG, A. (1989) 'Benefits and costs of dropout prevention in a high school program combining academic and vocational education: Third-year results from replications of the California Peninsula Academies', *Educational Evaluation and Policy Analysis*, 11, 4, pp. 405–16.

STERN, D., DAYTON, C., PAIK, I., WEISBERG, A. and EVANS, J. (1988) 'Combining academic and vocational courses in an integrated program to reduce high school dropout rates: Second-year results from replications of the California Peninsula Academies', *Educational Evaluation and Policy Analysis*, 10, 2, pp. 161–70.

STERN, D., MCMILLION, M., HOPKINS, C. and STONE, J.R. (1990) 'Work experience for students in high school and college', *Youth and Society*, 21, 3, pp. 355–89.

STERN, D. and NAKATA, Y. (1989) 'Characteristics of high school students' paid jobs, and employment experience after graduation', in STERN, D. and EICHORN, D. (Eds) *Adolescence and Work: Influences of Social Structure, Labor Markets, and Culture*, Hillsdale, NJ: Erlbaum.

STERN, D. and NAKATA, Y. (1991) 'Paid employment among US college students: Trends, effects, and possible causes', *Journal of Higher Education*, 62, 1, pp. 25–43.

STERN, D., RABY, M. and DAYTON, C. (1992) *Career Academies: Partnerships for Reconstructing American High Schools*, San Francisco, CA: Jossey-Bass.

STERN, D. and STEVENS, D. (1992) 'Analysis of unemployment insurance data on the relationship between high school cooperative education and subsequent employment', paper prepared for the National Assessment of Vocational Education, Berkeley, CA: School of Education, University of California.

STERN, D., STONE, J.R., HOPKINS, C. and MCMILLION, M. (1990) 'Quality of students' work experience and orientation toward work', *Youth and Society*, 22, 2, pp. 263–82.

STERN, D., STONE, J.R., HOPKINS, C., McMILLION, M. and CAGAMPANG, H. (1992) 'Quality of work experience as perceived by two-year college students in co-op and non-co-op jobs', *Journal of Cooperative Education*, 28, 1, pp. 34–47.

STERN, D., STONE, J.R., HOPKINS, C., McMILLION, M. and CRAIN, R. (1994) *School-Based Enterprise: Productive Learning in American High Schools*, San Francisco, CA: Jossey-Bass.

STEVENS, D.W. (1991) *Occupations and Earnings of Former Vocational Education Students: Research Design Issues*, Baltimore, MD: Merrick School of Business, University of Baltimore.

STEVENS, D.W. (1992) *Occupations and Earnings of Former Vocational Education Students: Progress Report*, Baltimore, MD: Merrick School of Business, University of Baltimore.

STEVENS, D.W. (1993) *The School to Work Transition of High School and Community College Vocational Program Completers: 1990–1992*, Baltimore, MD: Merrick School of Business, University of Baltimore.

STONE, J.R., STERN, D., HOPKINS, C. and McMILLION, M. (1990) 'Adolescents' perceptions of their work: School supervised and non-school supervised', *Journal of Vocational Education Research*, 15, 2, pp. 31–53.

STONE, J.R. and WONSER, R.L. (1990) *Alternative Strategies for Providing Work Experience*, St. Paul, MN: Minnesota Research and Development Center for Vocational Education, Department of Vocational and Technical Education, University of Minnesota.

STYLES, M.B. and MORROW, K.V. (1992) *Understanding How Youth and Elders Form Relationships: A Study of Four Linking Lifetimes Programs*, Philadelphia, PA: Public/Private Ventures.

SUCHORSKI, J.M. (1987) *Contract Training in Community Colleges, Seminar Paper*, University of Florida, (ERIC Document No. ED 291 425).

TAGGART, R. (1981) *A Fisherman's Guide: An Assessment of Training and Remediation Strategies*, Kalamazoo, MI: Upjohn Institute.

TAN, H. *et al.* (1991) *Youth Training in the United States, Britain, and Australia*, Santa Monica, CA: RAND.

TIERNEY, J.P. and BRANCH, A.Y. (1992) *College Students as Mentors for At-Risk Youth: A Study of Six Campus Partners in Learning Programs*, Philadelphia, PA: Public/Private Ventures.

TIFT, S.E. (1992) 'Youth apprenticeships: Can they work in America?', *EQW Issues*, October.

TILLMAN, R.L. (1990) 'A study of the ethical orientation of co-op students', *Journal of Cooperative Education*, 26, 3, pp. 15–29.

References

TUHOLSKI, R.J. (1982) 'Today's apprentices, tomorrow's leaders', *VocEd*, 57, 1.

US BUREAU OF THE CENSUS (1992) *Current Population Reports, Series P-60, No. 180. Money Income of Households, Families, and Persons in the United States: 1991*, Washington, DC: US Government Printing Office.

US CONGRESS, OFFICE OF TECHNOLOGY ASSESSMENT (1990) *Worker Training: Competing in the New International Economy*, Washington, DC: Government Printing Office.

US DEPARTMENT OF EDUCATION (1990) *Carl D. Perkins Vocational and Applied Technology Education Act of 1990. Part E: The Tech Prep Education Act*, Washington, DC: Government Printing Office.

US DEPARTMENT OF EDUCATION (1990) *One on One: A Guide for Establishing Mentor Programs*, Washington, DC: US Department of Education.

US DEPARTMENT OF LABOR (1989) *Building a Quality Workforce*, Washington, DC: GPO.

US DEPARTMENT OF LABOR, BUREAU OF LABOR STATISTICS (1984) *Employment Projections for 1995*, Washington, DC: GPO.

US DEPARTMENT OF LABOR, BUREAU OF LABOR STATISTICS (1991) *The Employment Situation: September, 1991. News Release*, USDL 91–498.

US DEPARTMENT OF LABOR, BUREAU OF LABOR STATISTICS (1992) *How Workers Get Their Training: 1991 Update. Bulletin 2407*, August.

US DEPARTMENT OF LABOR, BUREAU OF LABOR STATISTICS (1993a) *The Employment Situation: May 1993. News Release*, USDL 93–200.

US DEPARTMENT OF LABOR, BUREAU OF LABOR STATISTICS (1993b) *Work and Family: Changes in Wages and Benefits among Young Adults, Report 849*, July.

US DEPARTMENT OF LABOR, BUREAU OF LABOR STATISTICS (1993c) *Proportion of High School Graduates Enrolled in College Continued to Increase in 1992. News Release*, USDL 93–153, May.

US DEPARTMENT OF LABOR, EMPLOYMENT AND TRAINING ADMINISTRATION (1992b) *Dilemmas in Youth Employment Programming: Findings from the Youth Research and Technical Assistance Project, Volume I, Research and Evaluation Report Series 92-C*, Washington, DC: GPO.

US DEPARTMENT OF LABOR, EMPLOYMENT AND TRAINING ADMINISTRATION (1992a) *Economic Change and the American Workforce*, Washington, DC: GPO.

US GENERAL ACCOUNTING OFFICE (1990) *Training Strategies: Preparing Non-college Youth for Employment in the US and Foreign Countries*, Washington, DC: GPO.

US GENERAL ACCOUNTING OFFICE (1991) *Transition from School to Work:*

Linking Education and Worksite Training. (GAO/HRD-91-105), Washington, DC: GPO.

US GENERAL ACCOUNTING OFFICE (1992) *The Changing Workforce: Demographic Issues Facing the Federal Government*, Washington, DC: GPO.

US GENERAL ACCOUNTING OFFICE (1993) *Transition from School to Work: States Are Developing New Strategies to Prepare Students for Jobs*, (GAO/HRD-93-139). Washington, DC: GPO.

VEUM, J.R. and WEISS, A.B. (1993) 'Education and the work histories of young adults', *Monthly Labor Review*, April, pp. 11–20.

VICKERS, M. (1991) *Building a National System for School-to Work Transition: Lessons from Britain and Australia*, Cambridge, MA: Jobs for the Future.

VIRGINIA STATE COUNCIL OF HIGHER EDUCATION (1987) *An Assessment of Career Planning and Placement in Virginia's State-Supported Institutions of Higher Education*, Richmond, VA: VSCHE, (ERIC Document No. ED 291 417).

VON BORSTEL, F. (1982) 'Productive education: A comparative study of the present day experience in developing nations', doctoral thesis, Department of Educational Theory, University of Toronto, Canada.

WALKER, G. and VILELLA-VELEZ, F. (1992) *Anatomy of a Demonstration: The Summer Training Education Program (STEP) From Pilot Through Replication and Postprogram Impacts*, Public/Private Ventures, Philadelphia, PA.

WALL, M. and LUTHER, V. (1988) *Schools as Entrepreneurs: Helping Small Towns Survive*, Lincoln, NE: Heartland Center for Leadership Development.

WALSH, J. and BREGLIO, V.J. (1976) *An Assessment of School Supervised Work Education Programs. Part II: Urban Cooperative Education Programs and Followup Study (3 volumes)*, San Francisco, CA: Olympus Research Centers.

WEBER, J.M. (1987) *Strengthening Vocational Education's Role in Decreasing the Dropout Rate. Research and Development Series No. 267*, Columbus, OH: Center on Education and Training for Employment, Ohio State University.

WEINBERGER, S.G. (1992) *How to Start a Student Mentor Program. Fastback 333*, Bloomington, IN: Phi Delta Kappa Educational Foundation.

WEISMAN, J. (1991) 'Few businesses bolster training programs to make up for school shortfalls, poll finds', *Education Week*, 9 October, p. 5.

WENTLING, T.L. *et al.* (1991) *Technology and Preparation Pilot Test, Year 2, School Year 1990–91, Evaluation Report*. Indianapolis: Indiana State Dept. of Education, (ERIC Document No. ED 339 839).

WHITWORTH, L.L. (1982) 'New pathways to apprenticeship', *VocEd*, 57, 1, pp. 38–40.

WIGGINTON, E. (1986) *Sometimes a Shining Moment: The Foxfire Experience*, New York: Doubleday.

WILLIAM, T. GRANT FOUNDATION, COMMISSION ON WORK, FAMILY AND CITIZENSHIP (1988) *The Forgotten Half: Non-College Youth in America*, Washington, DC: Grant Foundation.

WILLIAM, T. GRANT FOUNDATION, COMMISSION ON WORK, FAMILY AND CITIZENSHIP (1992) 'The meaning of apprenticeship: When and how to use the term', *Student Apprenticeship News*, 1, 3, p. 6.

WILLIAMSON, H. (1989) 'Mini-enterprise in schools: The pupil's experience', *British Journal of Education and Work*, 3, 1, pp. 71–82.

WILLIS, R.J. and ROSEN, S. (1979) 'Education and self-selection', *Journal of Political Economy*, 87, 5, part 2, S7–S36.

WILSON, W.J. (1987) *The Truly Disadvantaged: The Inner City, the Underclass, and Public Policy*, Chicago, IL: University of Chicago Press.

WITTE, J.C. and KALLEBERG, A.L. (1992) 'Matching training and jobs: Lessons from the German vocational education system', paper presented at the annual meeting of the Population Association of America, Denver, Co May.

WOOLDRIDGE, R.L. (1988) 'A commentary on C. Parsons: The Bridge-Cooperative education for all high school students' in William T. Grant Foundation, *Youth and America's Future*, pp. 86–90.

YASUDA, K.E. (1990) *Working and Schooling Decisions: A Study of New Hampshire Teenage Labor Market Behavior and the Level of Educational Attainment*, Concord, NH: State Department of Employment Security.

Index